The Welsh Peaks

Plate 1 **Route 18**—Tryfan in winter raiment

W. A. Poucher, Hon. F.R.P.S

The Welsh Peaks

A pictorial guide to walking in this region and to the safe ascent of its principal mountain routes, with 250 photographs by the author, 15 maps and 56 routes.

Eleventh Edition

Frances Lincoln

Frances Lincoln Ltd
4 Torriano Mews
Torriano Avenue
London NW5 2RZ
www.franceslincoln.com

First published in Great Britain 1962 by Constable and Company Ltd
Copyright © 1962 by William Arthur Poucher
Tenth edition 1997
Eleventh edition re-originated from the original photographs and
published by Frances Lincoln in 2005

British Library Cataloguing in Publication data
A catalogue record for this book is available from the British Library.

Printed and bound in Singapore

ISBN 07112 2404 8

9 8 7 6 5 4 3 2 1

*Hillwalking and scrambling carry certain risks. If you have any doubts
about your ability to conduct these activities you should consider engaging a
qualified guide or instructor to lead you or to instruct you in the techniques
required to travel safely in the mountains. Your use of this book indicates
your assumption of the risks involved, and is an acknowledgement of your
own sole responsibility for your safety.*

Preface to the eleventh edition

The Welsh Peaks first appeared in 1962 under the Constable imprint which has been maintained until this eleventh edition which is published by Frances Lincoln, who with the technology now available have re-originated all the photographs, so improving their quality.

Whilst my late father was fit and vigorous, he visited the area on a regular basis and checked the routes for accuracy and amended this guide accordingly; since his death in 1988 this task has been undertaken by the well-known climber, mountain guide and author Nigel Shepherd who lives in northern Snowdonia.

In spite of the routes being updated, it is still possible for slight changes to appear due to erosion, rock falls and other natural causes and if such variations are noticied by a user of this guide it will be most helpful if they would let me know so that they can be included in any future edition of this work.

It should be noted that the Routes described and illustrated herein have been frequented over the years without objection, but they do not necessarily constitute Rights of Way. If in any doubt, the reader should contact the owner of the land and ask permission to cross it before embarking upon their walk. This is most important in view of the outbreaks of vandalism which have occurred in recent years and have resulted in damage to fences, hedges, gates, walls, cairns and shelters in mountain districts; this is not only deplorable but also contrary to the accepted Country Code.

I would draw readers attention to a booklet, *Tread Lightly*, produced by the British Mountaineering Council in co-operation with the Mountaineering Council of Scotland, with financial support from the Nature Conservancy Council. This booklet covers many aspects of the correct conduct on and around the fells which is summed up by the phrase: 'Take nothing but photographs, leave nothing but footprints.'

Finally, I would urge leaders of school and youth parties not to venture on these hills unless the weather is favourable; moreover, they should always insist upon everyone wearing boots and proper clothing and carrying the various items mentioned in the section devoted to equipment. If they do this they will not only reduce the risk of accidents, but also avoid the, often needless, call for Moutain rescue.

A suggestion for a route card appears opposite and its use by every walker and scrambler could help reduce the number of casualties on our peaks. Please report your route to your lodgings and do not deviate from it.

The fifteen maps are reproduced with the permission of John Bartholmew & Son Limited.

John Poucher
Gate Ghyll, High Brigham
Cockermouth, Cumbria
2005

After Mr Poucher's death in August 1988, at the age of 96, his son and daughter-in-law felt that as he had loved Snowdonia so much it would be appropriate for there to be some form of memorial to him in the area. So with the agreement of the Director, a memorial seat was presented to Plas y Brenin in Capel Curig, where it was placed in the gardens. The seat bears a plaque which reads:

IN MEMORY OF
WALTER POUCHER 1891–1988
A RENOWNED MOUNTAIN PHOTOGRAPHER
WHO LOVED THE WILD PLACES

The **route card** illustrated opposite was introduced by the Snowdonia National Park some years ago. It forms the basis of sound safety practice by informing others of your plans for the day. Should an accident befall you and you fail to return as planned the information will be invaluable to Rescue teams. This route card, or something similar, should be left with someone where you are staying. Do not forget to report back if you inadvertantly finish late and far away from your intended return point.

Leave word
when you go
on our hills

Names and Addresses: Home Address and Local Address	Route
Time and date of departure	Bad weather alternative
Place of Departure and registered number of vehicle (if any)	
Estimated time of return	Walking/Climbing (delete as necessary)

GO UP WELL EQUIPPED — TO COME BACK SAFELY

Please tick items carried

Emergency Food	Torch	Ice Axe
Waterproof Clothing	Whistle	Crampons
(colour:	Map	Polybag
Winter Clothing	Compass	First Aid
(colour:		

Please complete and leave with landlady, warden etc.
Ask landlady or warden to contact Police if you are overdue
PLEASE REPORT YOUR SAFE RETURN

Contents

Introductory notes

The coastal resorts of Wales have been a treasured venue for the holidaymaker for many decades, and with the increased interest in mountain walking and rock climbing Snowdonia too has achieved an immense popularity that is second to none in this country. But the remote and wild landscape of South and Mid-Wales has for some inexplicable reason escaped this attention, despite the magnificence of the scenery, the opportunities for hill walking in comparative solitude, and the possibility of ascents of varying difficulty on its innumerable crags and cliffs. I hope the information given in these pages will lead to a more extensive exploration of the whole of the Principality. Energetic young men and women who have a special predilection for hill country may well choose Snowdonia for their first visit, and on arrival they will raise their eyes to the peaks and imagine themselves standing by one of the summit cairns, inhaling the invigorating mountain air and scanning the valleys far below, the chain of engirdling hills and the distant glimmering seas. Come what may, they lose no time in setting out to climb one of them and on reaching their objective gain that satisfaction that comes only after the ardours of the ascent. It is highly probable that Snowdon will be their first conquest, not only because it is the monarch of Wales and the countryside as far north as Scotland, but also because they believe it will disclose the finest and most comprehensive panorama on account of its dominating altitude. On achieving this ambition, they quite naturally speculate upon the merits of the views from the other high peaks in the region, and after talking over the question with friends they will in all probability continue their exploration by climbing Tryfan, or walking over the Glyders, or perhaps even traversing the fine Nantlle Ridge, on their first vacation. On returning home they will often ponder over these experiences, and especially so if they have been captivated by the spirit and mystery of the hills. The map will doubtless be unfolded at frequent intervals, and by tracing the routes thereon they will re-live these happy times. If they climbed Snowdon by the Pyg Track, their thoughts will follow that pleasant route from Pen-y-Pass with Crib Goch rising into the sky ahead, their surprise at the fine view of Lliwedd on attaining Bwlch y Moch, the tramp along the stony undulating path with Yr Wyddfa in front and the sudden appearance of Glaslyn below, the scramble up the steep zigzags to the Col where the Snowdon Railway first comes into view, the walk along the edge of the cwm with Snowdon ahead and the exhilaration of finally standing on the large cairn on the roof of Wales with a whole kingdom spread out far below.

A closer inspection of the map will suggest to our friends several other routes to this lofty peak, and curiosity will induce them to speculate upon their respective merits. Would the Miners' Track have been more interesting? Perhaps it would have been more thrilling to have made the ascent from the beautiful Vale of Gwynant by the Watkin Path, or what of the more distant approaches from the Snowdon Ranger Youth Hostel or Rhyd-ddu? Then another line of thought may develop; for they had seen a grand array of peaks engirdling the horizon from Yr Wyddfa and they will speculate again upon the merits of the panoramas from their summits, to realise with surprise that a lifetime is not too long in which to become acquainted with them all.

The cogitations of our young friends will follow a normal course and they will do exactly the same as the rest of us did in our novitiate; for they will formulate the plans for their next holiday long before it is due. Next time they may decide to stay perhaps in Mid-Wales and explore the adjacent hills; but which ones? To solve this problem they will often get out the map, and while scanning it with happy anticipation compare it with the various guide-books which describe this lovely countryside. There they will read what their authors have so lucidly written, but much will inevitably be left to their imagination.

It is here that my long experience of the Welsh Peaks will help them to solve their problems, for by consulting this volume in conjunction with my other works devoted to this region they will not only be able to choose their centre with certainty, their routes to the peaks in the vicinity in accordance with their abilities, and their subjects for their cameras if they happen to be photographers, but they will also be able to see beforehand through the medium of my camera studies precisely the type of country that will satisfy every one of their needs. The mountains, whilst seemingly harsh, are a delicate environmental mix where man attempts to live in harmony with nature and nature strives to survive the onslaught. Inevitably the surge in popularity of mountain sports has taken its toll on the fragile existence of the wild places. Paths form and others become more eroded, leaving unsightly scars, unexplored and unknown corners become inundated with people and somehow the tranquillity becomes lost.

Everyone who visits the hills in this book, or mountains anywhere, must show respect for the natural and wild habitat they choose to enter and do all that they can to prolong and enhance the delicate beauty that, in the first instance, is so attractive.

Equipment

Anyone who ventures on to the hills without being properly equipped is foolhardy. The weather in the mountains can change rapidly and even in the summertime extremes of cold and heat may be encountered whilst out in the hills.

Footwear is of paramount importance. There are a number of considerations to be borne in mind when making a choice from the vast array of walking and climbing boots available. Cost is obviously important and it usually follows that the more expensive boots are likely to provide the user with longer use and greater comfort.

Walking boots must be sturdy and have a good sole. There are a variety of styles available in addition to the classic vibram pattern. Some lay claim to a host of uses in all variety of terrain and in truth there are few that don't match up to their sales hype. Be wary though of plastic soles on cheaper models or those that are notoriously slippery when used on wet rocks and grass.

There are two main types of upper available. The most satisfactory for longevity is without doubt leather. Carefully looked after and kept clean and well dubbined leather can be perfectly water-repellent. The more seams, and therefore stitching, there is in a boot, the more difficult it is to trust to its waterproofing. Water will find its way through even the tiniest of weaknesses and often the problem will not be the boot itself but the fact that water gets in through the top and the gaps along the lacing system.

There are numerous models made with tough nylon uppers. Material such as cordura is particularly hardwearing. Often, and certainly in the more expensive variety, they will include a breathable lining such as goretex. Many boots constructed in

Plate 2

this way claim impressive water repellency properties that over a period of long and hard use dwindles considerably. Proprietary cleaners and re-proofing substances are needed from time to time to increase the life of such footwear. There is a need to tread somewhat more carefully over sharp rocks as the material is easily damaged. This type of footwear is generally unsuited to walking in snowy conditions for they do not provide sufficient warmth or the rigidity required to kick steps and use crampons successfully.

For those who aspire to things other than walking and who might go scrambling along airy ridges and buttresses or rock climbing on cliff and crag, a more rigid boot may be found more suitable for tip-toeing on tiny edges. Such boots will differ from a walking boot in that they will have a stiffener inside the sole lending varying degrees of rigidity. A three quarter stiffener is perhaps the most versatile all round and a full shank for total stiffness as might be needed by the ice climber.

Readers will no doubt encounter plastic mountaineering boots in their quest to purchase. Normally these type of boots are for serious mountaineering in harsh winter conditions, the Alps and the highest mountains of the world. For the hillwalker they are totally unsuitable being cumbersome, overly warm and harsh on feet and knees.

Be sure to take good care of your feet at all times. Many modern boots require little or no breaking in period. For those that do make sure that at the first sign of any soreness you cover the part of your foot with plaster to prevent the formation of blisters. A stoic attitude in the face of soreness is foolishness because it may mean curtailment of a long planned holiday.

Waterproof clothing is an essential requirement for all who go into the hills. Being wet will turn a great day into one of continual misery and worse, may lead to hypothermia and the necessity for rescue. Nowadays there is little excuse for not having at least reasonably good waterproof or shell clothing, for there is wide choice not simply in mountaineering shops but also in the high street.

It does follow however that the best shell clothing for the job is generally to be found in specialist shops and there are a variety of waterproof but breathable materials that serve the hillwalker admirably. Cheaper garments made from proofed nylon in varying weights are perfectly adequate for mountain wear and suffer only from the problem of condensation build up on the inside of the garment. This may lead to a little discomfort and dampness but provided that the shell is worn all the time there will be no chilling effect from the wind.

Any good waterproof jacket should be well cut and allow freedom of movement. A large and accommodating hood is a good idea and one that closes snugly around the face but doesn't restrict vision is preferable. Such hoods will normally have a wired or at least stiffened visor. Pockets should be easily accessible whilst wearing a rucksack hipbelt and a large pocket to take a map is a worthy addition. Some jackets feature zipped underarm air vents. These are very useful in steamy conditions, when it is wet but warm. The sleeve closures must be convenient and it is a good idea to check that they can be easily done up with gloved hands.

A full length zip that operates in two directions is useful in that it provides good ventilation. A storm flap inside the zip will make it more weathertight. The alternative to a jacket is a pull over the head anorak or cagoule. This type of shell is clearly a more stormproof garment but lacks the ability to ventilate efficiently. At the end of the day it is largely a matter of personal choice and how deep into ones pocket one has to delve.

Many people comment on how unnecessary a pair of waterproof trousers is. One can only assume that such people have never spent time in the mountains in really wild weather. A large proportion of body heat is lost through the thighs and once wet, this loss is exaggerated considerably. Overtrousers are essential for comfort and well being. When choosing a pair ensure that you are able to get them on over the top of your walking boots. It's a good idea to buy a pair with a short knee length zip that facilitates this and it is possible to buy trousers with a full length zip that allows the wearer to take them on and off more easily. Trousers with a 'drop-seat' are convenient for a number of good reasons.

Fleece clothing is well established as an efficient insulator. A range of products is widely available and the prospective purchaser usually has a choice of differing weights and a bewildering array of patterns and colours. Fleece has the tremendous advantage over more traditional insulation such as wool, in that it retains warmth even when wet and that it dries out very quickly. It is not however, windproof, and can only be made so by additional shell clothing or as is more popular by a pertex covering. Jackets, jumpers and trousers are all available in fleece from all the top manufacturers.

Breeches are rarely seen these days having been largely superseded by a range of cotton/polyester trousers. Light-weight but very durable and often windproof, they are a rather more sensible alternative. For colder conditions long johns can be worn underneath or it may be preferable to resort to wearing fleece trousers when conditions become extremely cold.

Microfibre undergarments will be found to be a worthwhile addition to the winter wardrobe and may even be required at other times of the year. To achieve the most from such garments they should ideally be worn next to the skin and be quite a snug fit.

Gloves or mitts ought to be carried on all but the most reliable of summer days. Again there is tremendous choice from the cheapest to the most outrageously expensive. Fleece gloves or mitts are useful for the same reasons as previously mentioned but you might consider a windproof outer being worthwhile. Gloves made from waterproof breathable fabrics are only of any use if the material is fairly heavy. Woollen mitts such as the eternal Dachstein are particularly warm even when wet or completely frozen – unfortunately it is difficult to hold things with any security. It is worth considering wearing a lighter weight inner glove which can be used on its own in all but the coldest conditions.

Hats and balaclavas are also a necessity. Here once again, fleece is an efficient insulator. An outer covering of breathable waterproof material makes a hat both windproof and water resistant. Traditional woolly bobble hats are fine and so also is the mountaineers balaclava which folds up into a hat when you no longer need full head protection.

Gaiters are a covering for the lower part of the leg. Essentially they are worn to prevent snow from getting in to the top of the boot, melting and causing wet uncomfortable feet. They are equally applicable for use in the rain and when overtrousers are worn they will stop water percolating down the leg and into the top of the boot. Ordinary proofed nylon or waterproof breathable models are available.

A **Rucksack** will be needed to carry food and spare clothing that isn't being used. There is perhaps more choice available in rucksacks than any other single item of mountaineering equipment for in addition to the more well established marques there are a huge number of cheaper makes.

A rucksack for day use need not be too large. There is a saying among mountain folk that no matter what size sack you have you will nearly always fill it. That's no good at all if you have a 60 litre sac on a day trip. Normally, something around 25 to 30 litres will be more than adequate. In this size, the range is perhaps largest and the final choice must be left to the individual purchaser. Few rucksacks are waterproof though some claim to be, and it is usually necessary to place items inside a polythene bag inside the pack. Outside pockets are useful for storing things to which quick access is required, particularly water bottles on hot days and if your chosen rucksack has a lid it is likely to have an integrated pocket.

Other essential equipment includes a **compass**. The Silva

compass is by far and away the most common though there are other makes. Whichever compass you choose it should have a large base plate which enables you to measure long distances on the map. **Maps** are available in two useful scales. For general use a 1:50000 scale is adequate and for fine detail navigation a larger scale 1:25000 will be necessary. The Ordnance Survey produce large scale maps to all of the popular mountain regions of Wales and details of those required will be found in the introduction to each region. More about the compass and map appears under the chapter on navigation.

A **whistle, emergency bivvy bag, head torch** and **first aid kit** will complete the basic equipment required for safe travel in our hills and these can be supplemented with safety equipment necessary for winter walking or for scrambling and rock climbing.

List of equipment for summer hill walking
Boots.
Waterproof shell clothing. Jacket and Trousers.
Fleece jumper and spare. Wool is an alternative.
Warm hat and gloves or mitts.
Cotton trousers or breeches with long socks.
Some food and emergency food.
A flask or if it is a hot summer's day, a water bottle.
A map, compass and whistle.
Emergency bivvy bag.
Small first aid kit.
Gaiters.
Head torch.

Winter supplement
Warm undergarments.
Mitts or gloves and spares.
Lightweight insulated jacket or waistcoat.
Balaclava.
Ice axe and crampons.

Rock climbing and scrambling

North Wales is resplendent with precipitous cliffs of sound rock that have become the treasured playground of the rock climber. Those of Clogwyn du'r Arddu, Lliwedd, Craig yr Ysfa, Cwm Silyn, Llanberis Pass, Glyder Fach and Cwm Idwal afford climbs of varying difficulty and during fine weekends and holidays are immensely popular. Climbing areas in South and Mid-Wales are fewer but no less important.

Mountain scrambling falls into a category somewhere between walking and rock climbing. It is enormously popular and much information on out of the way scrambles is available. On many scrambles it is not necessary to have recourse to use the rope but there are those that offer a high degree of exposure where the consequences of a fall might be very serious. The judicious use of a rope is to be recommended in such places and it is necessary to have some training in the most appropriate techniques.

There are thus ample opportunities for the enjoyment of this exhilarating pastime among Welsh Peaks, but a novice would be well advised not to venture forth alone without proper guidance and training. There are a number of ways to be introduced to the sport. One is to go out with friends who have a good deal of experience and another is to enrol on a course run by qualified instructors.

Details of all the courses available that are run by bona fide and qualified personnel are contained in a brochure published annually by the British Mountaineering Council. Their address is 177–179 Burton Road, West Didsbury, Manchester M20 2BB. You can also get details of courses run by members of the British Association of Mountain Guides from their office in North Wales. The address is Plas y Brenin, Capel Curig, Gwynedd LL24 0ET.

Situated in a unique and wonderful setting, Plas y Brenin is one of two National Mountain Centres in Britain. The other is in Scotland. Owned and operated by the Sports Council the facility is there for anyone to take advantage of the expertise of the instructors. A whole variety of courses are available.

Joining a club is also a good way to be introduced to the hills and many of the more famous mountaineers have graduated from such traditional beginnings. One advantage of joining a club is that you will always be able to have contact with like minded people. This is particularly useful if you live far away from the hills. Many clubs also have huts and there are innumerable club huts from the most basic to the most comfortable, in Wales. The Climbers' Club has perhaps the widest choice. Quite often clubs will have a reciprocal arrangement with other clubs who own huts in different mountain areas. Any information you would like on joining a club is available directly from the BMC under whose wing all reputable clubs are affiliated.

This book is mainly concerned with walks and easy scrambles that will not normally require a rope but you will doubtless be inspired by the steeper and more craggy places you see on your travels around Wales and perhaps one day desire to venture forth on to more airy places. . . .

The Welsh Centres

The following list outlines the principal centres from which the Welsh Peaks may be most conveniently climbed. But it should be borne in mind that strong walkers are often able to reach them from more distant places. There are numerous hostels and other types of accommodation in Wales, but only those giving reasonably easy access to the major hill ranges are mentioned here. Since this region is so vast, the centres are described under three well-defined mountain areas:

Snowdonia

Betws y Coed is the Gateway to Snowdonia for perhaps the majority of visitors, and is well situated on the River Conwy at an important road junction. It has also the advantage of a railway connection with Llandudno Junction on the main line from the rest of Britain. Most of the region can be explored by motorists based in one of its many hotels. Roads lead into the heart of the mountains and penetrate the sylvan stretches of the Lledr Valley. It is too far away to be a really convenient centre for those without a car but in the summer there is a bus service to most parts of the park.

    Capel Curig is exceptionally well placed at the road junction to Llanberis and Bethesda and is an excellent centre for the walker. There are some comfortable hotels, a couple of guest houses and a Youth Hostel. All the starting points of routes are readily accessible to the motorist and buses serve many of them too during the summer months. Moel Siabod rises almost overhead and the eastern tops of the Carneddau and Glyders are only a short step away.

    Idwal Cottage is situated at the foot of Llyn Ogwen and on the crest of Nant Ffrancon. It stands in the very shadow of the peaks and affords easy access to the Carneddau, Tryfan, Idwal and the whole of the Glyders.

Bethesda is situated at the foot of Nant Ffrancon and has an hotel. It is too far away from the main peaks for the average pedestrian, but those who wish to be near the western Glyders and the south-western Carneddau will find it a good centre.

Pen y Gwryd is perhaps the most famous centre in the whole of Snowdonia, and stands at the junction of the roads to Llanberis and Beddgelert. It is encircled by the lower slopes of Snowdon, the Glyders and Moel Siabod, and thus gives easy access to many of their peaks. The hotel has a long mountaineering history and will always be closely associated with early pioneers of the sport.

Pen y Pass is equally well known and is superbly situated on the lofty crest of the Llanberis Pass. It is the starting point for the Snowdon Horseshoe, for other favoured routes to Yr Wyddfa, for the direct ascent of Glyder Fawr and Esgair Felen, and gives easy access to Llyn Llydaw. The name of the distinguished mountaineer Geoffrey Winthrop Young will always be associated with it and also with his famous Easter parties. It is now a Youth Hostel and Restaurant and there is a large car park nearby for over one hundred vehicles.

Llanberis stands on the shore of Llyn Padarn at the foot of the Llanberis Pass and may be reached by bus from Caernarfon and Bangor. It is the starting point of the Snowdon Railway, has several good hotels and guest houses, and there is a Youth Hostel on the mountainside above the town. It is the best centre for those making the long ascent to Yr Wyddfa by the well-trodden Llanberis Path, and also gives ready access to the frowning cliffs of Clogwyn Du'r Arddu.

Beddgelert spans the Afon Glaslyn at the junction of the main roads leading to Caernarfon, Portmadoc and Capel Curig and has several comfortable hotels and guest houses. The village is surrounded by the lower slopes of Snowdon and the southern satellites of Moel Siabod, while it is almost overshadowed by the fine peak of Moel Hebog. It is also within reasonable distance of Aberglaslyn Pass, and with the paths ascending the south side of Yr Wyddfa. The Nantlle Ridge is too far away for the average pedestrian, but may be reached by car or bus. Some six kilometres up the beautiful Vale of Gwynant stands the Youth Hostel of Bryn Gwynant, splendidly situated in a delightful sylvan setting overlooking the lake, while the guest house of the Holiday Fellowship is not far distant. Both are well placed for the ascent of Snowdon by the Watkin Path.

The **Snowdon Ranger** is a Youth Hostel and is pleasantly situated on the shore of Llyn Cwellyn. The path to Yr Wyddfa, well known as the Snowdon Ranger, starts from its very door and may be the oldest route on this mountain. It is also well placed for access to the Nantlle Ridge and to Mynydd Mawr, which rises on the other side of the lake. It may be conveniently reached by bus from Caernarfon or Beddgelert. There is a small car park opposite the starting point.

Mid-Wales

Dolgellau is centrally situated amid this vast area of peaks, which are so widely spread that those who stay here must use a car to reach them. It has some good hotels and there is a smaller one at Cross Foxes. The Youth Hostel of Kings is six kilometres away in the direction of Arthog. The town is well placed for the ascent of Cadair Idris by the famous Foxes' Path, for the rock traverse of the shattered ridge of Cyfrwy, and also gives easy access to the Precipice and Torrent Walks, two of the scenic gems in this district.

Tal y Llyn is the most romantically situated centre in Mid Wales and its two small but comfortable hotels stand at the foot of a sequestered lake that is completely enclosed by hills. It is the ideal starting point for the ascent of Cadair Idris by way of Cwm Cau, one of the wildest in the Principality, and also for the ascent of the Pencoed Pillar, a nice problem for the rock climber.

Dinas Mawddwy has one hotel and is the only convenient centre for pedestrians wishing to make the most interesting ascent of the Arans. The key to this walk is the hamlet of Abercywarch, about 1.5 kilometres to the north of the town, from where Cae Peris is reached by a narrow and twisting farm road giving access not only to the path to the two peaks but also to Craig Cywarch a well known crag of interest to the rock climber.

Bala occupies a splendid position at the northern extremity of Llyn Tegid, but its hotels and guest houses are rather distant from the Arans and Arennigs, although strong walkers may attain the summits of either group in a long day. Those who can find accommodation in Llanuwchllyn, a village at the southern extremity of Bala Lake, will be better placed for the ascents of both ranges and especially so for Aran Benllyn, which is the nearer of the two.

Harlech is the nearest centre with adequate hotel accommodation and a Youth Hostel for those wishing to explore the Harlech Dome. It is a rugged backbone of bare mountains in the hinterland, in which the Roman Steps and the Rhinogs afford the toughest and most attractive walking. Those having a car at their disposal may drive along the road to Barmouth and turn off to the left at Llanbedr, where a narrow and twisting lane gives access to one or other of the starting points that will be indicated later in this volume.

Llanbedr is a better centre for pedestrians undertaking the above expeditions, and there is a small hotel in the village.

Barmouth is an attractive seaside resort lying at the base of the southern slopes of the Harlech Dome, but is too far distant for the ascent of these peaks unless a car can be used for the long approach. The local scenic highlight is the famous Panorama Walk, which reveals fine views of the Mawddach Estuary below, backed by the precipitous front of Cadair Idris.

The Devil's Bridge is some nineteen kilometres to the east of Aberystwyth and has a splendidly situated hotel overlooking the deep wooded stretches of the Rheidol Valley, from which it may be conveniently explored. It is a good though distant centre for the ascent of Plynlimon, when transport is desirable to reach the starting points of this walk. But pedestrians may secure accommodation at the Dyffryn Castell Inn which lies at the foot of this immense sprawling mountain and the well marked track to its summit is five and a half kilometres in length. Accommodation may also be found at Eisteddfa Gurig for the shorter route of ascent and there is a good hotel in Ponterwyd and a Youth Hostel at Ystumtuen.

South Wales

Abergavenny has hotels and guest houses and is a convenient centre for motorists who wish to penetrate the deep valleys of the Black Mountains. Their bare, whaleback ridges afford excellent walking country to the north of the town. There is a Youth Hostel at Capel y Min.

Crickhowell also has hotels, and some motorists may prefer to stay here for these pleasant drives. There is a Youth Hostel in the town.

Talgarth has one hotel and is the nearest town to the lofty Gadair Ridge which dominates the Black Mountains. Its crest may be most easily attained from the tiny adjacent hamlet of Pen y Genfford.

Hay on Wye lies in the Wye Valley to the north of the range and has two small hotels which are rather distant for the average pedestrian.

Brecon is the only centre with hotel accommodation near the Brecon Beacons, and a car is useful for those who wish to make the complete traverse of the lofty ridge that is dominated by Pen y Fan, the most picturesque peak in this range. There is a Youth Hostel at Ty'n y Caeau, to the east of the town.

Storey Arms is the nearest starting point for Pen y Fan and is some 14 kilometres from Brecon. It stands on the crest of the mountain road connecting this town with Merthyr Tydfil and may be reached from either by bus. The nearest accommodation is a Youth Hostel at Llwyn y Celyn, three kilometres distant.

Trecastle has the nearest hotel to Carmarthen Fan and there is a Youth Hostel at Llanddeusant. The starting point of the ascent is 32 kilometres from Brecon which has ample accommodation.

Glossary of Welsh place-names

Readers who do not speak the Welsh language may have some difficulty in understanding the various place-names given to the different topographical features of the Principality. I hope, therefore, the translation of some of them as set out below will be useful to travellers and climbers in this delectable country.

Aber, a river mouth
Ach, water
Aderyn, a bird
Ael, a brow or edge
Afon, a river
Allt, a wooded slope
Aran, a high place
Arddu, a black crag

Bach, little
Bala, a lake outlet
Ban, peak, crest, beacon
Bedd, a grave
Ber, a hilltop
Bera }
Bere } beak, top, point
Betws, a chapel
Beudy, a byre or cowhouse
Blaen, the head of a valley
Boch, a cheek
Bod, a home or abode
Bont, a bridge
Braich, an arm or branch
Bran, a crow

Bras, thick or fat
Brith, speckled
Bron, the slope of a hill
Brwynog, marshy
Bryn, a hill
Bwlch, a pass
Bychan, small

Cadair, a chair or throne
Cae, an enclosed field
Caer, a camp or fortress
Cafn, a trough
Canol, middle
Capel, a chapel
Carn, a cairn or heap of stones
Carnedd, a cairn
Carreg, stone
Caseg, a mare
Castell, a castle or fortress
Cau, a hollow
Cefn, a ridge
Celyn, holly
Cidwm, a wolf

Clogwyn, a cliff or precipice
Clwyd, a gate
Clyd, a shelter
Cnicht, a knight
Coch, red
Coed, a wood
Congl, a corner
Cors, a bog or swamp
Craig, a rock or crag
Crib, a ridge or jagged edge
Cribin, the small crest of a
   hill
Croes, a cross
Crug, a mound
Cwm, a hollow or coombe
Cwn, dogs
Cymer, a confluence

Dau, two
Dinas, a natural fortress
Dol, a dale or meadow
Drosgl, a rough hill
Drum, a ridge
Drws, a door
Du or *ddu*, black
Dwr, water
Dyffryn, a wide valley
Dysgl, a dish or plate

Eglwys, a church
Eigiau, a shoal of fish
Eira, snow
Erw, an acre
Eryri, a highland
Esgair, a shank or limb

Fach, small
Faes, a field or meadow
Fan, peak, crest, beacon
Fawr, large
Felin, a mill
Ffordd, a road
Ffynnon, a well or fountain
Foel, a bare or bald hill
Fyny, upwards

Gaer, a camp
Gafr, a goat
Gallt, a slope
Ganol, middle
Gardd, a garden
Garn, an eminence
Garth, an enclosure
Gawr, a torrent
Glas, blue-green
Gludair, a heap
Glyn, a deep valley
Goch, red
Golau, a light or beacon
Golwg, a view
Gors, a swamp
Grach, scabby
Groes, a cross
Grug, heather
Gwastad, a plain
Gwern, an alder coppice
Gwyn, white
Gwynt, wind

Hafod, a summer dwelling
Hebog, a hawk

Helgi, a hunting dog
Helyg, willows
Hen, old
Heulog, sunny
Hir, long
Hydd, a stag

Isaf, lower

Las, blue-green
Llan, a church
Llech, a flat stone
Llefn, smooth
Llithrig, slippery
Lloer, moon
Llwyd, grey
Llwyn, a grove
Llyn, a lake
Llys, a hall
Lon, a lane

Maen, a block of stone
Maes, a field or meadow
Man, a place
Mawr, large
Meirch, horses
Melin, a mill
Melyn, yellow
Mign, a bog
Min, lip or edge
Mir, fair
Moch, pigs
Moel, a bare or bald hill
Mor, sea
Morfa, flat seashore – sea fen

Mur, a wall
Mynach, a monk
Mynydd, a mountain

Nant, a brook
Newydd, new

Oer, cold
Og, harrow
Ogof, a cave
Oleu, light
Onn, an ash tree

Pair, a cauldron
Pant, a hollow
Parc, an enclosure
Pen, a peak or top
Penrhyn, a promontory
Pentre, a village
Perfedd, centre
Perth, a hedgerow bush
Pistyll, the spout of a
    waterfall
Plas, a mansion
Poeth, hot
Pont, a bridge
Porth, a port, gateway
Pwll, a pool

Rhaeadr, a waterfall
Rhiw, hill or slope
Rhyd, a passage or ford
Rhyn, a cape

Saeth, an arrow
Sarn, a causeway

Silin, spawn
Sych, dry

Tal, end
Tan, under
Tir, soil
Tomen, a mound
Traeth, sandy shore
Tref, a town
Tri, three
Trum, a ridge
Twll, a cavern
Twr, a tower
Ty, a house
Tyddyn, a small farmstead

Uchaf, upper or higher

Un, one

Waun, moorland
Wen, white
Wern, an alder swamp
Wrach, a witch
Wrth, near

Y – Yr, the
Yn, in
Ynys, an island
Ysfa, a sheep walk
Ysgol, a ladder
Ysgubor, a barn
Ystrad, a street or sale
Ystum, a curve or bend
Ystwyth, winding

The Welsh Peaks
Routes of ascent

The Snowdon Group Map 1

The Glyders Group Map 2
GLYDER FAWR

Heights of the principal Welsh Peaks

Arranged in order of altitude, in metres and feet above sea level, with their mountain group.

1	Yr Wyddfa	1085	3559	Snowdon
2	Crib y Ddysgl	1065	3494	Snowdon
3	Carnedd Llywelyn	1064	3490	Carneddau
4	Carnedd Dafydd	1044	3426	Carneddau
5	Glyder Fawr	999	3277	Glyders
6	Glyder Fach	994	3261	Glyders
7	Pen yr Ole Wen	978	3208	Carneddau
8	Foel Grach	976	3202	Carneddau
9	Yr Elen	962	3156	Carneddau
10	Y Garn	947	3106	Glyders
11	Foel Fras	942	3091	Carneddau
12	Elidir Fawr	924	3031	Glyders
13	Crib Goch	923	3028	Snowdon
14	Tryfan	915	3002	Glyders
15	Aran Fawddwy	905	2969	Arans
16	Lliwedd	898	2946	Snowdon
17	Pen y Gadair	893	2929	Cadair Idris
18	Pen y Fan	886	2906	Brecon Beacons
19	Aran Benllyn	885	2903	Arans
20	Yr Aryg	876	2875	Carneddau
21	Corn Du	873	2864	Brecon Beacons
22	Moel Siabod	872	2860	Moel Siabod
23	Mynydd Moel	863	2831	Cadair Idris
24	Arenig Fawr	854	2801	Arenigs
25	Llwytmor	849	2785	Carneddau
26	Pen yr Helgi-du	833	2732	Carneddau
27	Foel Goch	831	2726	Glyders
28	Carnedd y Filiast	821	2693	Glyders
29	Mynydd Perfedd	812	2664	Glyders
30	Waun Fach	811	2660	Black Mountains
31	Nameless	805	2641	Glyders

32	Bannau Brycheiniog	802	2632	Carmarthen Fan
33	Pen y Gadair Fawr	800	2624	Black Mountains
34	Pen Llithrig y Wrach	799	2621	Carneddau
35	Cribyn	795	2608	Brecon Beacons
36	Moel Hebog	782	2565	Moel Hebog
37	Elidir Fach	782	2564	Glyders
38	Craig Cywarch	779	2557	Arans
39	Drum	770	2526	Carneddau
40	Moelwyn Mawr	770	2526	Moel Siabod
41	Gallt yr Ogof	763	2503	Glyders
42	Y Llethr	756	2480	Harlech Dome
43	Pen Plynlimon Fawr	752	2468	Plynlimon
44	Moel Llyfnant	751	2463	Arenigs
45	Diffwys	750	2460	Harlech Dome
46	Yr Aran	747	2450	Snowdon
47	Craig Eigiau	735	2411	Carneddau
48	Craig Cwm Silyn	734	2408	Nantlle Ridge
49	Drysgol	730	2397	Arans
50	Moel Eilio	726	2381	Snowdon
51	Rhinog Fawr	720	2362	Harlech Dome
52	Pen Allt Mawr	719	2358	Black Mountains
53	Rhinog Fach	712	2335	Harlech Dome
54	Moelwyn Bach	710	2329	Moel Siabod
55	Trum y Ddysgl	709	2326	Moel Hebog
56	Garnedd Goch	700	2296	Moel Hebog
57	Mynydd Mawr	698	2290	Moel Hebog
58	Allt Fawr	698	2290	Moel Siabog
59	Cnicht	689	2260	Moel Siabog
60	Arenig Fach	689	2260	Arenigs
61	Creigiau Gleision	678	2224	Carneddau
62	Moel Druman	676	2217	Moel Siabod
63	Moel Cynghorion	674	2211	Snowdon
64	Tyrau Mawr	661	2168	Cadair Idris
65	Moel yr Ogof	655	2148	Moel Hebog
66	Mynydd Tal y Mignedd	653	2142	Nantlle Ridge

67	Moel yr Hydd	648	2125	Moel Siabod
68	Gyrn Wigau	643	2109	Carneddau
69	Moel Lefn	638	2094	Moel Hebog
70	Y Garn II	633	2076	Nantlle Ridge
71	Pen y Castell	620	2034	Carneddau
72	Gallt y Wenallt	619	2030	Snowdon
73	Tal y Fan	610	2001	Carneddau

The principal Welsh lakes

This list includes the more important lakes viewed from the routes to the peaks. They are in alphabetical order under each mountain group and their height in metres and feet above sea level is given, together with their approximate position.

Snowdon

Bwlch Cwm Llan	510	1673	Col between Yr Aran & Bwlch Main
Coch	519	1705	Cwm Clogwyn
D'ur Arddu	579	1901	Cwm Brwynog
Fynnon y Gwas	420	1381	Cwm Treweunydd
Glas	652	2139	Cwm Glas
Glas	519	1705	Cwm Clogwyn
Glaslyn	600	1971	Cwm Dyli
Gwynant	66	217	Vale of Gwynant
Llydaw	431	1416	Cwm Dyli
Nadroedd	519	1705	Cwm Clogwyn
Teyrn	377	1237	Cwm Dyli

Glyders

Bochlwyd	550	1806	Between Tryfan & Y Gribin
Caseg Ffraith	742	2434	Above Cwm Tryfan
Cwm y Ffynnon	382	1254	N of Pen y Pass
Y Cwn	711	2280	S of Devil's Kitchen
Idwal	372	1223	Cwm Idwal
Padarn	256	840	N of Llanberis
Peris	256	840	E of Llanberis

Carneddau

Cowlyd	355	1165	N of Capel Curig
Crafnant	183	603	NE of Capel Curig

Dulyn	532	1747	Cwm Griafolen E of Carnedd Llewelyn
Eigiau	371	1219	N of Capel Curig
Ffynnon Llyfant	830	2725	E of Carnedd Llewelyn
Fynnon Lloer	650	2085	N of Llyn Ogwen
Fynnon Llugwy	544	1786	N of Helyg
Geirionydd	187	616	NW of Betws y Coed
Melynllyn	638	2094	Cwm Griafolen
Ogwen	299	984	Crest of Nant Ffrancon

Moel Siabod

Yr Adar	571	1874	NE of Cnicht
Y Biswail	570	1871	N end of Cnicht Ridge
Croesor	520	1706	N of Moelwyn Mawr
Cwm Corsiog	540	1771	N of Lyn Croesor
Dinas	53	176	Vale of Gwynant
Diwaunydd	368	1208	SE of Pen y Gwryd
Edno	547	1797	N of Cnicht
Y Foel	535	1756	E of Moel Siabod
Llagi	377	1238	N of Cnicht
Mymbyr	179	588	Capel Curig
Pen y Gwryd	271	890	Pen y Gwryd

Moel Hebog

Cwellyn	141	464	E of Mynydd Mawr
Cwm Silyn	336	1105	W end of Nantlle Ridge
Dywarchen	234	770	NW of Rhyd Ddu
Y Gadair	182	598	S of Rhyd Ddu
Nantlle Uchaf	98	322	W end of Drws y Coed

Cadair Idris

Y Cau	473	1552	S of Pen y Gadair
Y Gadair	560	1837	N of Pen y Gadair
Tal y Llyn	80	270	S of Dolgellau

Harlech Dome

Arddyn	313	1029	E of Llawr Llech
Y Bi	450	1476	S of Rhinog Fach
Bodlyn	379	1245	E of Diffwys
Cwm Bychan	184	605	Below Roman Steps
Du	520	1706	N of Rhinog Fawr
Dulyn	540	1771	S of Y Llethr
Gloyw	390	1279	NW of Rhinog Fawr
Hywel	540	1771	S of Rhinog Fach
Morwynion	410	1345	Bwlch Tyddiad
Perfeddau	470	1542	NW of Y Llethr

Arrenigs

| Arenig Fawr | 404 | 1326 | S of Llyn Celyn |

The Arans

| Tegid (Bala) | 161 | 530 | N of Aran Benllyn |
| Creiglyn Dyfi | 579 | 1900 | E of Aran Fawddwy |

Plynlimon

| Llygad Rheidol | 500 | 1640 | Due N of summit |

Black Mountains

| Grwyn Fawr | 495 | 1627 | NE of Gadair Ridge |

Brecon Beacons

| Cwm Llwch | 570 | 1870 | NW of Corn Du |

Camarthen Fan

| Llyn y Fan Fawr | 600 | 1968 | E of summit |
| Llyn y Fan Fach | 500 | 1640 | W of summit |

Mountain photography

I have already written and lectured extensively on this fascinating branch of photography, and in my *Snowdon Holiday* I included copious notes on its application to the mountains of North Wales. But since this work has been out of print for many years, it may be useful to deal more fully with the subject herein than I did in its companion volume, *The Lakeland Peaks*. These notes are written largely for the benefit of keen photographers with an interest in both black and white and in colour photography.

1 **The ideal camera for the mountaineer** is undoubtedly the modern miniature owing to its compact form, quick manipulation, great depth of focus, variable zoom lenses and lightness in weight. While these instruments are represented in their very best and most expensive type by the Leica, Pentax and Nikon series, it does not follow that other less costly makes will not give good photographs. Many of these cheaper cameras will give perfectly good results for those who require their camera to provide them with pictures of the most poignant moments of their holiday. The great joy of such equipment is that it is foolproof in use and so long as you remember to keep your finger away from the lens you will have good pictures. For the more discerning photographer, those who require greater flexibility in choosing aperture and shutter speed, an SLR camera with a zoom lens or a variety of fixed focus lenses is essential. Here too it is possible to obtain fully automated cameras that require little more than a point and click technique – the winding on of the film frame is even done for you. Such cameras are heavily reliant on battery power and in the event of battery failure may not work at all.

2 **The lens** is the most important feature, and the best of them naturally facilitate the perfect rendering of the subject. A wide aperture is not essential, because it is seldom necessary to work out of doors at anything greater than F/4.5. It is advisable to use the objective at infinity in mountain photography because overall sharpness is then obtained, and to stop down where required to bring the foreground into focus. It is in this connection that the cheaper camera, which of course is fitted with an inexpensive lens, falls short of its more costly competitors; for the latter are corrected for every known fault and the resulting photographs are then not only more acceptable for enlarged reproduction but also yield exhibition prints of superlative quality. Three lenses are desirable in this branch of photography: 1. a 28mm or 35mm wide angle; 2. a standard 50mm which is usually supplied with most cameras; and 3. a long focus lens such as a 135mm or even a 200mm. These cover every likely requirement: the wide angle is most useful when on a mountain or lofty ridge; the 50mm encompasses the average scene, such as hill and valley; and the long focus is an advantage when the subject is very distant. An analysis of their use in the photographs in this book is as follows:

Wide angle 50 per cent
Standard 40 per cent
Long focus 10 per cent

It is possible to obtain extremely high quality zoom lenses that incorporate all of the above focal lengths. This is quite obviously an advantage in that it not only means carrying less weight and bulk but that it also facilitates the accurate framing of the picture without having to change lenses.

3 A **lens hood** is an indispensable accessory, because it cuts out adventitious light and increases the brilliance and clarity of the picture. Many people have the illusion that this gadget is only required when the sun is shining and that it is used to keep the direct rays out of the lens when facing the light

source. While its use is then imperative, they often overlook the fact that light is reflected from many points of the hemisphere around the optical axis, and it is the interception of this incidental light that is important.

4 A **filter** is desirable, especially for the good rendering of skyscapes. For black and white photography a pale orange yields the most dramatic results, providing there are not vast areas of trees in the landscape in which all detail would be lost. It is safer to use a yellow filter, which does not suffer from this defect, and with autumn colours a green filter is very effective. The exposure factors do not differ materially, and in view of the wide latitude of modern black-and-white film the resulting slight differences in density can be corrected when printing.

For colour work a skylight filter is essential for reducing the intensity of the blues and for eliminating haze. Many people also like to use a polarising filter which can enhance a picture by making light waves vibrate in a single plane. This is particularly useful when there is light from many directions such as reflections off water or more obviously, from snow.

5 The choice of **film** is wide. For straightforward colour print photography a film with an ASA rating of 100 will be sufficient for almost everything that you need. For more dreary light faster speeds up to 400ASA may be useful. Transparency, or slide, film yields excellent results and there is again, a wide choice. Some films such as Kodachrome and Fujichrome include processing in the price whereas there are others that do not. Processing for such films is by the E6 process and if this is your chosen medium you should try to find a company that produces excellent results for they do vary.

Black and white film is available in similar ratings and those that work with this medium will appreciate the subtleties that it offers both in the latitude of the film and in the creation of pictures in the darkroom.

A basic point to remember about any film, is that the faster the ASA rating the more 'grainy' a picture becomes. Though this factor will not be noticeable on a small scale, it will become all too apparent the larger a picture is blown up.

6 **Exposure** is important when taking a picture but is not relevant to those cameras where the photographer has no control over the aperture and shutter speed.

A slow shutter speed will necessitate holding the camera very steady. If you are using a long or heavy lens it may be preferable to put it on a tripod. A fast shutter speed will capture images and freeze them even though it may be a moving object. A minimum shutter speed of 125/sec is a yardstick from which to work.

The aperture determines how much of the scene will be in focus. The smaller the aperture is the more you will have of the picture in focus. If you are taking pictures of far away scenes it is not so important to consider the aperture. If however, you would like to take a picture that includes some close foreground detail, such as your companion, you will require a greater depth of focus and a smaller aperture will be necessary. (In photography terms this is called Depth of Field). An aperture of F/8 is a versatile minimum to work with.

The most successful pictures are the result of a carefully considered combination of shutter speed and aperture.

7 **The best time of year** for photography among the Welsh Peaks is the month of May. A limpid atmosphere and fine cumulus are then a common occurrence and less time is wasted in waiting for suitable lighting. Colour work at this time is also satisfactory because the landscape still reveals the reds of the dead bracken, which, however, disappear in June with the rapid growth of the new fresh green fronds. Nevertheless, the most dramatic colour pictures are obtained during the last week in October because the newly dead bracken is then a

Plate 3 Cloud over the Glyders and Tryfan, seen from Crimpiau

fiery red, the grass has turned to golden yellow, and the long shadows increase the contrast between peak and valley.

8 **Lack of sharpness** is a problem that causes disappointment and though one is often apt to blame the lens, the complaint is in fact due to camera shake. It is one thing to hold the instrument steady at ground level with a good stance and no strong wind to disturb the balance, while it is quite another problem in the boisterous breezes on the lofty ridges of Wales. When these conditions prevail, it is risky to use a slow shutter speed and maximum stability may be achieved by leaning against a slab of rock or, in a terrific gale of wind, by lying down and jamming the elbows into the spaces between the rocks; but foreground should never be sacrificed on this account. In calm weather a light tripod may be used, but in all other conditions it is too risky to erect one and have it blown over a precipice!

9 **Lighting** is the key to fine mountain photography, and the sun at an angle of 45 degrees, over the left or right shoulder, will yield the required contrasts. These conditions usually appertain in the early morning or the late evening. If possible avoid exposures at midday with the sun overhead when the lighting is flat and uninteresting. Before starting on any outing, study the topography of your mountain so that full advantage can be taken of the lighting. Moreover, never be persuaded to discard your camera when setting out in bad weather, because the atmosphere in the hills is subject to the most sudden and unexpected changes, and sometimes wet mornings develop into fine afternoons, with magnificent clouds and limpid lighting. If your camera is then away back in your lodgings, you may live to regret the omission.

10 **The Sky** is often the saving feature in mountain photographs since cloudless conditions or a sunless landscape seldom yield a pleasing picture. See plate 3.

11 **Haze** is one of the bugbears in this branch of photography, and these conditions are especially prevalent among the Welsh Peaks during July and August. If an opalescent effect is desired, this is the time of year to secure it, but while such camera studies may be favoured by the purist, they seldom appeal to the photographer who prefers to see the detail he or she knows exists in the subjects.

12 **Design or composition** is the most outstanding feature of a good camera study; that is, one that not only immediately appeals to the eye, but rather one that can be lived with afterwards. Everything I have so far written herein on this subject comes within the scope of technique, and anyone who is prepared to give it adequate study and practice should be able to produce a satisfying picture. But to create a picture that far transcends even the best snapshot requires more than this and might well be described as a flair, or if you like, a seeing eye that immediately appreciates the artistic merits of a particular mountain scene. And strangely enough those who possess this rare gift usually produce a certain type of picture which is indelibly stamped with their personality; so much so that it is often possible to name the photographer as soon as the work is displayed. And, moreover, while this especial artistic trait may be developed after long application of the basic principles of composition, the fact remains that it is not the camera that really matters for it is merely a tool, but the person behind the viewfinder, who, when satisfied with the design of the subject, ultimately and quite happily releases the shutter.

To the painter, composition is relatively easy, because it can be made to conform to the basic principles of art by moving a tree to one side of the picture, or by completely removing a house from the foreground, or by inducing a stream to flow in another direction, or by accentuating the real subject, if it happens to be a mountain, by moving it or by increasing or decreasing its angles to suit their tastes. Photographers on the other hand have to move themselves and the camera here and there in order to get these objects in the right position in the viewfinder. When you move to one side to improve the position of one of them, another is thrown out of place, or perhaps the lighting is altered. In many cases, therefore, a compromise is the only solution, because if too much time is spent in solving his problem the mood may change, and the opportunity could be lost. It is just this element in mountain photography that brings it into line with sport, and, like golf, it can be both interesting and exasperating. Of course, the critic can sit in a comfortable chair by a warm fire at home and pull a photograph to pieces. He or she may not, perhaps, realise that the person taking the picture may have been wandering about knee-deep in a slimy bog, or that a bitterly cold wind was sweeping across a lofty ridge and making the teeth chatter, or that the light was failing, or that they had crawled out on a rocky spur with a hundred-foot drop on either side to get the subject properly composed.

Assuming, therefore, both lighting and cloudscape are favourable, what are the essential features of good composition? In the first place, you must select a pleasing object that is accented by tonal contrast as the centre of interest; in the second, you must place this object in the most attractive position in the frame or picture space: and in the third, you must choose a strong and appropriate foreground. Or, in other words, when the weather is favourable the success or failure of your photograph will depend entirely upon the viewpoint.

Thus, if your subject happens to be Snowdon, I may be able to help you with a few hints about five of the illustrations in this book. It is generally agreed that the eastern aspect of this mountain is the finest and it looks its best up to noon on a sunny morning with cloud drifting overhead. But you must first decide whether you wish to make a picture of the majestic peak itself, or of the whole range; if the former, there is one

Plate 4 Snowdon from Llyn Llydaw

Plate 5 The Snowdon Group from Garth Bridge

Plate 6 Snowdon from the Royal Bridge, Capel Curig

Plate 7 Snowdon from the Pinaccles of Capel Curig

matchless viewpoint, whereas if the latter, there are at least three and each one of them has a different type of foreground. Let us begin with the peak itself, whose tonal contrast will be enhanced by side lighting; whose strongest placing in a vertical frame will be in the centre of the picture space, as in a horizontal frame in the upper right-hand third as in plate 4; and whose most appropriate foreground will be Llyn Llydaw. Now, you must remember that it is always the foreground that leads the eye into a picture, and the treatment of the lake is therefore of the utmost importance. In the first place, the distant shore must never form a horizontal line above the lower third; for if you place it in the centre it will cut the picture into two halves. Moreover, some bold rocks on the near shore will add strength and interest to the whole study, and if you have a friend with you, ask them to stand near the shore to impart scale to the picture. The beauty of the graceful lines of the Snowdon group always delights the eye and one of the nearest viewpoints that reveal them to advantage is Garth Bridge, above the little waterfall that enters the western end of Llynnau Mymbyr. The turbulent stream above the bridge, dappled with rocks and embellished by a single tree on the right, makes an excellent foreground for this photograph, as shown in plate 5. If you retreat farther from the range you will find another charming foreground in the Royal Bridge at the foot of Llynnau Mymbyr, but since Snowdon is now some ten miles distant its imposing character will be diminished if you do not use a long-focus lens. This allows the group to fill the frame completely and in your picture it will assume a similar magnitude to that seen by the eye, as seen in plate 6. A higher viewpoint has certain advantages and you will find one by walking up to the Pinnacles of Capel Curig. From the lowest of them you will secure a splendid photograph in which the twin lakes and Plas-y-Brenin yield a satisfactory foreground which leads the eye in one vast sweep to this magnificent mountain range, as shown in plate 7. Finally, whenever you take a shot of any of the

Welsh Peaks, remember that it will be improved not only by placing a lake, a stream, a bridge a figure or a group of climbers in the foreground, but also on occasion by introducing a tree or cottage or some object whose size, if known, will impart both interest and scale to your picture.

Note
1. In case readers are interested in the photographic equipment used by my father, I can disclose that on the many occasions he was asked this question, his reply was 'Since the availability of 35mm film I have always used Leica cameras, replacing them as new models appeared.' In his last years he used an M2 with 35, 50 and 90mm lenses for monochrome with Kodak Plus X film; for colour work he used a Leicaflex with 28, 50, 90 and 135mm lenses, plus a 45/90mm zoom, in conjunction with his favourite Koachrome 25.

2. Some years before my father died he presented the collection of black and white negatives he had amassed over a period of more than half a century to the Royal Photographic Society and they now form part of their archive. They wish it to be known that prints from these can be supplied for an appropriate fee.

John Poucher

Photography in the different groups

I have often been asked "What is the best view *of* such and such a mountain?" or "what is the most striking view *from* so and so?" These are difficult questions, because the answers depend so much upon one's personal tastes, which are influenced in no small degree by atmospheric conditions on any particular occasion. The present volume seems to be a convenient medium for an attempt to offer some guidance on this very debatable question, and while there are doubtless many who will disagree with my opinions, I shall give them for what they are worth. Where possible I have appended references to appropriate examples already portrayed in one or other of my works, as follows:

SL: *Snowdonia through the Lens*
SH: *Snowdon Holiday*
WW: *Wanderings in Wales*
EH: *Escape to the Hills*
WP: *The Welsh Peaks* (the present work)

The number indicates the plate in the particular volume, to which I have added the most suitable time of day for photographing the subject (G.M.T). It should be noted that the examples given were not necessarily taken at the best time or season.

The suggestions are arranged according to the grouping system adopted throughout this work and under two headings: (1) the best pictorial views *of* the groups or their separate tops; (2) The most striking views *from* the groups. After what I have already written herein it will be obvious that foreground interest is of paramount importance since it bears a distinct relationship to the pictorial rendering of the main subject.

The best pictorial views of the group
The eastern aspect of Snowdon
(*a*) From Llyn Llydaw before noon. SL 1; SH 52; EH 203; WP 4 & 18.
(*b*) From Crib Goch before noon. SH 57; EH 208; WP 12.

(c) From Garth Bridge before noon. WP 5.

(d) From Llynnau Mymbyr any time of day. SL jacket; EH 1; EH 176.

(e) From the Royal Bridge before noon. SL 5; EH 169; WP 6.

(f) From the Pinnacles of Capel Curig before noon. WP7.

The western aspect of Snowdon

(a) From Y Garn II after 2 p.m. SH 43; WP 184 & 187.

(b) From Craig y Bera and Mynydd Mawr after 2 p.m. WP 202

The northern aspect of Snowdon

(a) From the Glyders before noon. SL 34, WP 79.

(b) From Llyn Padarn after 4 p.m. WP 55.

(c) From Y Garn after 4 p.m. WP 109.

Crib Goch

(a) From Pen y Pass before 11 a.m. SL 51; EH 207.

(b) From Crib y Ddysgl after 2 p.m. SL 53; WP 13.

(c) From Cwm Glas after 3 p.m. SH 1; WP 62.

Lliwedd

(a) From Llyn Llydaw before 10 a.m. SH 66.

(b) From the Snowdon Horseshoe after 4 p.m. SH 68; EH 213; WP 11.

Yr Aran

From Llyn Gwynant before 11 a.m. SL 42; WW 202; WP 33.

The Glyders

From upper Nant Ffrancon after 4 p.m.

Tryfan

(a) From Helyg before 11 a.m. SL 14; SH 76; sunset SL 61; WP 85.

(b) From Caseg-fraith Ridge before 11 a.m. SL 27; WP 1 & 86.

Bristly Ridge

From Llyn Caseg-fraith before 11 a.m. SL 28; WW 188; EH 192; WP 89.

Cwm Idwal

From Pen yr Ole Wen after 5 p.m. summer. SL 23; WP 147.

Y Garn
From head of Llyn Ogwen before 11 a.m. WP 106.

Carneddau
(*a*) From the Pinnacles of Capel Curig before noon. SL 12.
(*b*) Craig yr Ysfa from Cwm Eigiau before 11 a.m. SH 7; WP 134.
(*c*) Black Ladders from Carnedd Dafydd after 4 p.m. WP 143.

Moel Siabod
(*a*) From near the Ugly House before noon. SL 10.
(*b*) From the path to Llyn Crafnant before 11 a.m.
(*c*) From Crimpiau 4 p.m.

Cnicht
From Tan Lan after 3 p.m. EH 187; SH 35; WP 160.

The Moelwyns
From the Afon Glaslyn after 3 p.m. WW 178; WP 174.

Moel Hebog
(*a*) From Llyn Dinas before noon. SL 44.
(*b*) From the Afon Glaslyn before noon. EH 198.
(*c*) From Pont Cae'r-gors after 5 p.m. SH 33.
(*d*) Y Garn II and Craig y Bera from Llyn y Gadair before 11 a.m. WP 185.
(*e*) Craig y Bera from Llyn y Dywarchen before noon. WP 199.
(*f*) Mynydd Mawr from the Snowdon Ranger before 11 a.m. WP 48.
(*g*) Mynydd Mawr from Waun-fawr after 3 p.m. WP 204.

Cadair Idris
(*a*) From the north after 5 p.m. summer, WW 104; WP 205.
(*b*) Craig y Cau from the east before 111 a.m. WW 106; WP 207.
(*c*) Pen y Gadair from Cyfryw after 3 p.m. WW 109; WP 211.

The Harlech Dome
(*a*) From the east before 11 a.m. WW 1545; WP 213.
(*b*) Rhinog Fach from Llyn Hywel after noon. WW 161; WP 216.

The Arenigs
From the north-west after 4 p.m. ww 148.

The Arans
(*a*) From Bala Lake after 5 p.m. ww 135.
(*b*) Aran Benllyn from Drysgol before noon. ww 125; wp 223.

Plynlimon
(*a*) From the south any time of day. wp 227.
(*b*) From Eisteddfa Gurig before noon. ww 91; wp 230.

The Black Mountains
From Skirrid Fawr before 11 a.m. ww 24; wp 231.

The Brecon Beacons
(*a*) From the Golf Course at Cradoc in later afternoon. wp 235.
(*b*) Pen y fan from Cribyn before noon. ww 24; wp 237.

Carmarthen Fan
(*a*) Eastern escarpment from the Standing Stone in the morning wp 240.
(*b*) North Western Cwms from Sport Height 458 in the afternoon.

The most striking views from the groups
Snowdon
(*a*) The Glyders and Crib Goch up to 3 p.m. sl 54; wp 14.
(*b*) Lliwedd and Llyn Llydaw after 4 p.m. sh 65; wp 15.

Crib Goch
(*a*) The Horseshoe before noon. sh 57; wp 12.
(*b*) The Ridge and Pen y Pass up to 3 p.m. sh 61.
(*c*) Llyn Glas and the Llanberis Lakes up to noon. sh 62.

Clogwyn station
Llanberis Pass any time of day. wp 57.

Yr Aran
(*a*) The South Ridge of Snowdon up to 2 p.m. ww 201; wp 34.

(*b*) Moel Siabod and Llyn Gwynant about noon. ww 203; wp 37.

(*c*) Mynydd Mawr and Llyn Cwellyn before noon. ww 204; wp 36.

The Glyders

(*a*) Tryfan from Llyn Caseg-fraith before noon. wp 88.

(*b*) Snowdon and the Castle of the Winds before 11 a.m. sl 43; wp 79.

(*c*) The Devil's Kitchen from above after 4 p.m. sl 39; wp 102.

(*d*) Cwm Glas from Esgair Felen after 4 p.m. sh 46; wp 98.

(*e*) The Glyders from Y Garn after 2 p.m. wp 110.

Carneddau

(*a*) Sunset from Carnedd Llywelyn, 5 p.m. onwards sl. 26; wp 138.

(*b*) Snowdon and Cwm Idwal from Pen yr Ole Wen after 5 p.m. summer. wp 147.

(*c*) Tryfan and Llyn Ogwen from Pen yr Ole Wen after 3 p.m.

(*d*) Ogwen Valley from Crimpiau before noon. wp 117.

(*e*) Llyn Crafnant from Crimpiau all day. sl 4: wp 116.

Moel Siabod

(*a*) Western panorama comprising Moel Hebog and Snowdon before noon. wp 156.

(*b*) Cwm Dyli from Clogwyn Bwlch-y-maen in the morning.

(*c*) Snowdon Horseshoe from Llyn Edno up to 2 p.m. sh 21; wp 162.

(*d*) Snowdonia panorama from Cnicht any time of day. wp 164, 165 & 166.

Moel Hebog

(*a*) Beddgelert and the vale of Gwynant up to 3 p.m. sh 32; eh 197; wp 182.

(*b*) Snowdon from Y Garn II after 2 p.m. sh 43; wp 184 & 187.

(*c*) Snowdon from Craig y Bera after noon. wp 202.

(*d*) Nantlle Ridge from Craig Cwmsilin any time of day. wp 194.

Cadair Idris
(a) Snowdon and the Harlech Dome from Cyfwry all day. ww 110; wp 209.
(b) Mawddach Estuary from Cyfrwy all day. ww 111; wp 210

The Harlech Dome
(a) The ridge from Rhinog Fawr after 2 p.m. ww 159; wp 214.
(b) Y Llethr from above Llyn Hywel after 2 p.m. ww 163; wp 218.

The Arenigs
Panorama of Snowdonia and Mid-Wales all day.

The Arans
Cadair Idris from Aran Fawddwy before noon.

The Brecon Beacons
(a) Corn Du from Pen y fan in the morning. ww 36; wp 238.
(b) Llyn Cwm-llwch from Corn Du in the morning. ww 37; wp 239.

Carmarthen Fan
(a) The Brecon Beacons in the afternoon. wp 246.

Notes on the Routes

I have divided the Welsh Peaks into *thirteen Mountain Groups* for the sake of convenience and easy reference. They commence with Snowdon because it is the highest mountain in the Principality and its ascent the most esteemed. The groups in this particular part of the region follow each other in clockwise sequence and end with the Moel Hebog range. *The Routes* to the dominating peak in each group are also arranged clockwise wherever possible so that they fit into the general scheme and thus avoid undue cross reference. This arrangement facilitates the choice of those routes which are more or less adjacent, as for instance the Rhyd Ddu Path and the Snowdon Ranger, where one of them can be ascended and the other descended. But I have purposely omitted any description of the *Descents* because when the ascents are reversed they obviously answer this requirement. *The Panorama* from the reigning peak in each group is always described at the termination of its first ascent. Many of the routes involve the traverse of subsidiary tops and the conspicuous features revealed from them are noted in passing, despite the fact that there may be a similarity in the views when the peaks are near together.

Farther south, however, I have not been able to follow this scheme because the ranges are more scattered. I have therefore first given details of Cadair Idris since it is the most popular peak and terminated the descriptions with that of Carmarthen Fan, which is one of the least known mountains in Wales.

Many of these attractive ranges have been sadly neglected by walkers, perhaps because they are less spectacular than those in North Wales. I have therefore described and illustrated only the route which discloses the finest topography in each group, but in many of them the terrain is relatively easy and other ways of reaching the summits may be worked out on the spot with little risk.

Mountain navigation

The skills required to navigate safely and accurately are won only after long apprenticeship. Like many aspects of the mountaineers craft you would be well advised to seek expert instruction in techniques by going on a course or by going out with experienced friends.

The basic tools required are a map and compass. The map is the single most important for without it a compass is worth little. Time should be spent studying the map and learning how mountain features are interpreted by the map makers. Contour lines are the most complex to understand for they show shape and form of the hills, the steepness and height above sea level. Learning to read contour lines will help you to create an image in your mind's eye of what the mountains will look like. Once out in the field apply your interpretation to what you actually see and discover whether or not the two match up.

When using the map to identify features you should try to work with it set so that if the map was true to life size you could lie it over the ground and all features would match both on the ground and the map. This is called *orientating the map*. Inevitably this will entail reading the map upside down or even from the side but it will make it considerably easier to understand.

You must also familiarise yourself with the various ways in which roads and footpaths, lakes and rivers and all manner of other things are shown. There are two scales of map that are of interest to the walker. One is the 2cm to 1 kilometre scale OS Landranger series (1:50000) and the other the 4cm to 1 kilometre (1:25000) OS Outdoor Leisure series. The latter scale, being somewhat larger, affords the mountain navigator much more detail both in contour and crag features and also by showing walls and fences.

The compass is an integral part of the toolkit and the most commonly used, by far, is the Silva type 4. For the compass to be of any use it should have a long baseplate with a metric measuring scale and a device called a roamer which splits grid squares on the map into tenths enabling the user to work out grid references accurately. The magnetic needle of the compass is contained in the compass housing – a circular housing marked off in degrees from 0 to 360 and correspondingly marked N, S, E and W. The compass housing must also have a set of parallel lines underneath that are called orientating lines. A small magnifying glass incorporated into the base plate is a useful extra tool for identifying vague features on the map.

In order to take a bearing from one point to another you must follow some basic steps. *STEP 1* Line up an edge of the compass along the intended direction of travel. The compass housing should be at the starting end of the journey with the direction of travel arrow pointing to where you want to go. *STEP 2* Hold the compass firmly in place and turn the compass housing until the red orientating lines on the base of the housing are parallel with the grid lines that run vertically up the map (the Eastings). There is an arrow joining the middle two lines and this should point to the top of the map. *STEP 3* Take the compass off the map and add on the magnetic variation. In N Wales in 1996 it was 4.5 degrees. It decreases by about 0.5 degree every four years. *STEP 4* Hold the compass in front of you and turn until you line the red part of the magnetic compass needle up with the North mark on the compass housing rim. The direction to walk in is the one where the direction of travel arrow points.

This is a very basic explanation of the technique and if you are unsure of how to operate it you must seek expert advice before you can expect to rely on it in a life or death situation.

It is not enough simply to be capable of performing the previously mentioned tasks. Successful navigation relies on what can best be described as 'mountain sense'. This is a feeling and an awareness for the things that are around you combined with sensible and logical thought processes and close attention to detail.

You will also need to know how to measure distances along the ground. This is most accurately done by pace counting. An average person will take about 60–65 double paces to 100 metres over easy walking ground. The rougher it is the more you might take. Learning the skill of pacing can only be done through a great deal of practice but it can become a reliable aid to successful navigation. Pacing and timing go together though the latter, due to countless stops to check map and compass, can be difficult to use accurately and is at best a rough guide.

To work out how long it will take to cover a certain distance you must consider both the length of the journey and the height gained. If no height is gained you normally would only consider the distance. However, if the going is rough it may occasionally take more time to descend than it would to ascend.

As a foundation from which to work take an average walking pace of 1 kilometre every 12 minutes (1.2 minutes per 100 metres) and add 1.5 minutes for every 10 metre contour line crossed in ascent. Thus, if you have a section of your journey to cover that is 1500 metres long and goes from the 200 metre contour to the 360 metre contour, you have;

Distance 15 x 1.2 t 18 minutes
Height gain 16 x 1.5 t 24 minutes
Total time for the section = 42 minutes

In terms of measuring the distance whilst walking one would multiply ones own average number of paces per 100 metres by 15. It is always better to count in units of 100 metres because it is difficult to keep track of the running total when a large figure is involved. Pebbles or a special click counter are useful aids to remembering how far you have gone.

If you become lost or dis-orientated, which you inevitably will sometimes, try not to become too flustered. There are some important basics to staying safe. Do not follow streams or ravines over steep ground and try to avoid having to find your way down ground interspersed with crags and cliffs. Open grass slopes are much safer.

Since this book will be read by men and women of all ages, these figures may be discouraging to those in advancing years so it may be useful to give an account of a trip around the Snowdon Horseshoe on May 8th 1956. I was in my sixty-fifth year and at 10 am a young friend and I left Pen y Pass after a previous day of heavy rain. It was a cold sunny invigorating morning and we never hurried anywhere but reached Bwlch y Moch in an hour and Crib Goch at noon. We left the cairn half an hour later and stood on the summit of Snowdon at 2pm where we spent a lazy hour in resting and refreshment. We passed the stony top of Lliwedd at 4pm and were back at our starting point at 6pm. Thus taking eight leisurely hours for this wonderful walk. I already possessed a good collection of photographs of the Horseshoe, but on this occasion took a further twenty four shots in monochrome and a similar number in colour, all of which involved time spent in discovering unusual viewpoints. So, to those of you in your sixties and seventies, I say, Have a Go!

MOUNTAIN RESCUE

If you or your companion sustains an injury that is incapacitating seek shelter at the earliest opportunity. Here your emergency clothing, survival bag and spare food will come in useful. Try to identify your position on the map and mark it down. You could accost passing fellow walkers to fetch help but if you need to leave anyone behind to go for help yourself make sure you know where the rescue team can find them. Go to a telephone box and dial 999 and ask for mountain rescue. If you decide that it is foolish to move you can try to attract attention by using the International Distress signal which is six long flashes or whistle blasts followed by a minute's pause and then repeated. The reply is similar but flashes or blasts are only three.

Detailed Directions for 56 Routes
The Snowdon Group

Yr Wyddfa	1085 metres	3559 feet
Crib y Ddysgl	1065 metres	3494 feet
Bwlch Glas (zigzags)	993 metres	3258 feet
Crib Goch	923 metres	3028 feet
Lliwedd	898 metres	2946 feet
Bwlch Coch	858 metres	2816 feet
Bwlch y Saethau	820 metres	2691 feet
Yr Aran	747 metres	2450 feet
Moel Eilio	726 metres	2381 feet
Moel Cynghorion	674 metres	2211 feet
Gallt y Wenallt	619 metres	2030 feet
Bwlch y Moch	586 metres	1925 feet
Bwlch Cwm Brwynog	495 metres	1625 feet

OS Map: Landranger 115 Snowdonia
                Outdoor Leisure 17 Snowdon & Conwy Valley

It is only right and proper that Snowdon should assume pride of place in the following pages, not so much because it is the dominating peak of Wales, but more especially as its elevation is perhaps the finest in the Principality and most of the routes to its summit admit of little variation. All of them are clearly defined throughout and five traverse lofty ridges for part of the way. It is scarcely surprising that the most popular starting point is Pen y Pass, since Routes 1 and 4 together form the famous Horseshoe, a ridge "walk" that is full of interest all the way and reveals the mountain at its best. The Llanberis Path is usually regarded as the easiest, those of the Snowdon Ranger and Watkin Path are a little harder, and that from Pen y Pass by way of Crib Goch is the steepest of them all. All the routes

Plate 8 Crib Goch from Pen y Pass. Starting point for **Routes 1, 2, 3, 4 and 10**

Map 1
The Snowdon Group

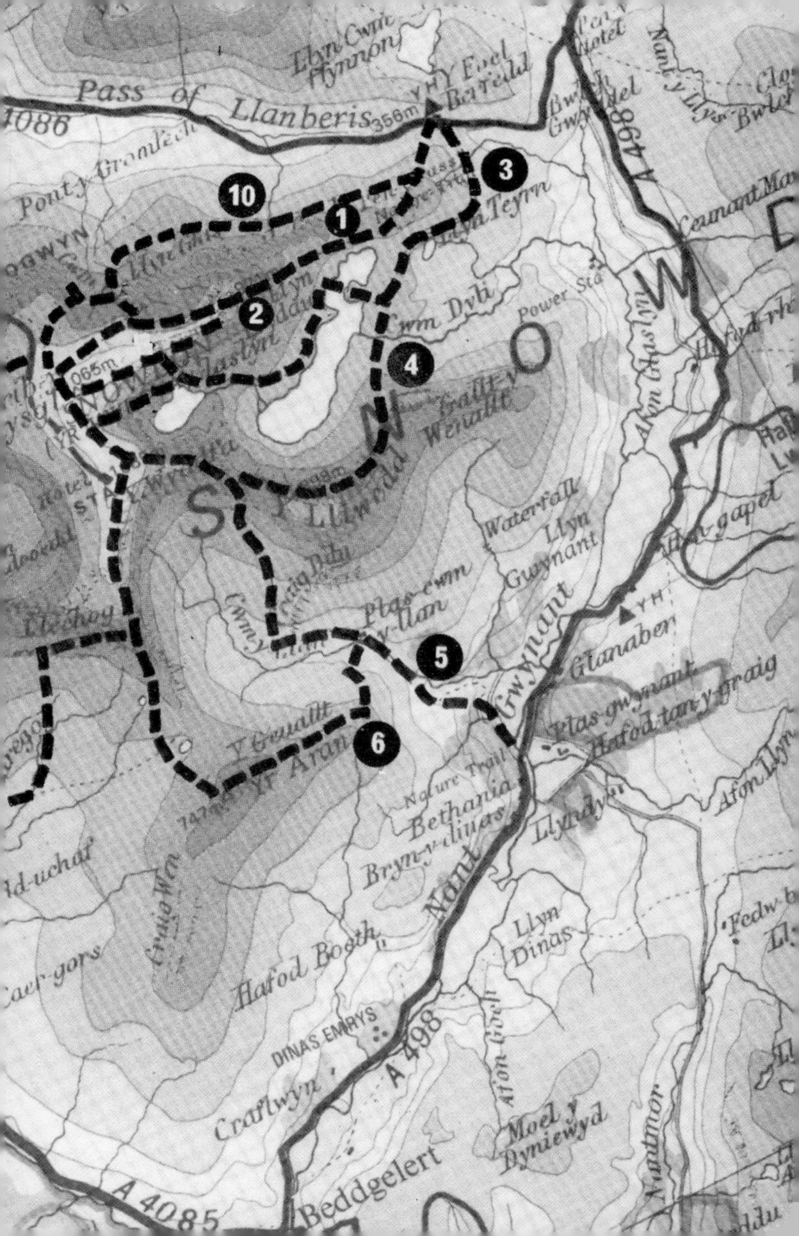

Pass of Llanberis
4086
358m
Llyn Cwm Ffynnon
Pont-y-Gromlech
10
1
2
3
4
5
6
Cwm Dyli
Power Sta
1065m
Llyn Teyrn
Afon Glaslyn
A 498
Nant y Llys
Bwlch
Llydaw
Waterfall
Llyn Gwynant
Plas-cwm-y-llan
Plas-gwynant
Hafod-tan-y-graig
Glanaben
Y Gwaliit
Yr Aran
Nature Trail
Bethania
Gwynant
Nant
Llyn Dinas
Hafod Booth
Caer-gors
DINAS EMRYS
Craflwyn
Afon Goch
Moel y Dyniewyd
Beddgelert
A 4085
Nantmor
Afon Llynedd
Allt-y-gapel
S
N
O
W
D

described and illustrated herein are so well trodden that even in misty weather they should present no great difficulties. Whereas in snow and mist they should be left severely alone by all but the most experienced winter walkers, especially so if snow lies on ice as this treacherous condition is often the cause of accidents in the most unsuspected places.

Snowdon Route 1. Pen y Pass and Crib Goch. Leave the car park below the crest of the Llanberis Pass GR 647555 and follow the higher track which starts under the electricity pole, as waymarked; it rises along the northern flanks of the *Last Nail in the Horseshoe* right up to Bwlch y Moch. After passing through a collection of gigantic boulders it swings round left into a shallow valley. This is the junction for the rather indistinct path over to the right which eventually leads into Cwm Glas (see route 10). Ahead rises the broad, stony track to Bwlch y Moch, with Crib Goch towering overhead all the way. On attaining the pass GR 634553 the route forks; the left branch is the Pyg Track and the right branch our route to Crib Goch. At this point there is a fine view into Cwm Dyli, with Lliwedd on its far side and Llyn Llydaw below. Our well-trodden path now steepens and while gaining height winds in and out of several rocky outcrops until, with the disappearance of grass, it begins to rise sharply. Ahead there is one tricky bit that is almost vertical, but reliable hand-holds and footholds give sufficient pull to pass this hazard safely. Beyond it well travelled marks lead upwards to the rocky staircase which eventually emerges by the cairn on our first summit.

The spacious prospect from Crib Goch is electrifying in its magnificence; for ahead the narrow rock ridge undulates as far as the Pinnacles which are crowned by the noble cone of Yr Wyddfa. To the L of the reigning peak the ridge falls to Bwlch y Saethau and then rises again to Lliwedd whose cliffs descend steeply to Llyn Llydaw far below. To the R, and beyond the Pinnacles, the ridge rises in steps from Bwlch Coch to Crib y

Ddysgl, with the zigzags on its L and the Parson's Nose below on its R. Farther to the R there is a bird's-eye view into Cwm Glas, with its tiny lake cupped in the base of the hollow, and beyond it a distant view of the Llanberis Lakes. Still farther to the R rise the chain of the Glyders, separated from this lofty perch by the deep Llanberis Pass, whose road may be perceived as a thin white line far below.

Some 400 yards of knife edge leads to the Pinnacles, but those with a steady head will experience no difficulties in crossing it in calm weather. These obstacles may be traversed by means of ample hand and footholds, but those who prefer to avoid them may pass below the sharp crest. Bwlch Coch is soon encountered, with views on the L of Glaslyn at the foot of Yr Wyddfa. Route 10 arrives at this point from Llyn Glas down to the R. From here the track rises along the crest of the ridge, ascends an easy chimney on the R, and emerges immediately below Crib y Ddysgl. There are several paths on this broad shoulder, but do not take the one on the right because it leads to the top of the Parson's Nose, a cliff only suitable for experienced rock climbers. Beyond the summit of Garnedd Ugain the track descends gently and swings round to the left to the large finger stone at Bwlch Glas, the exit of the zigzags, and here the railway is encountered and followed to the summit of Snowdon. On a clear day the immense panorama unfolded from the large cairn on Snowdon is one of the finest in Britain, and despite the fact that it is possible to pick out the coast of Eire, the Isle of Man and Scafell Pike, in Lakeland, these objects are too far away to hold the gaze of the walker, and unconsciously ones eye is drawn to the more attractive and closer detail of the landscape in the shape of the spurs of Snowdon itself. Of these it is perhaps the sheer cliffs of Lliwedd that first attract the eye, but since the sun is always on the wrong side of this peak for its full appraisal, it is only natural to turn to view the ridge just traversed enclosing the blue-green waters of Glaslyn far below. It may well be that Crib

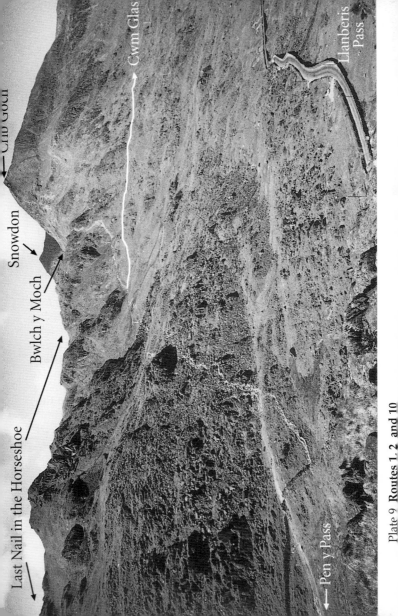

Crib Goch

Cwm Glas

Llanberis Pass

Snowdon

Bwlch y Moch

Last Nail in the Horseshoe

Pen y Pass

Plate 9 **Routes 1, 2 and 10**

Plate 10 **Routes 1 and 2**

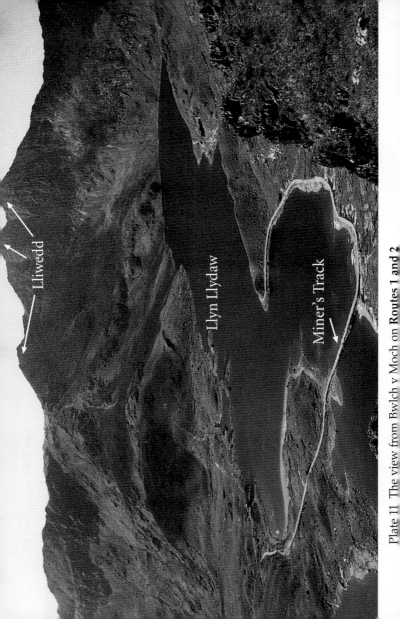

Plate 11 The view from Bwlch y Moch on **Routes 1 and 2**

Goch will rivet your attention by reason of its diminutive appearance, as it looks a long way below although there is a difference in altitude of barely 200 metres. Beyond the ridge rising to Crib y Ddysgl the solitude of the Glyders appears tremendous and beyond them again there is a glimpse of Carnedd Llywelyn and Pen yr Ole Wen. To the east the twin Capel lakes catch the light at the foot of Moel Siabod, and on swinging round to the south the cliffs of Cadair Idris stand out on the far horizon. Nearer at hand and in the south-west Moel Hebog is prominent, and the ridges of this group trail away to the north to end with the bold and compact form of Mynydd Mawr. The circle is completed with the glint of light on Llyn Cwellyn, R of which Moel Eilio leads the eye to the flat expanse of Anglesey and the sea. It is always inspiring to stand on the highest peak south of Scotland and to scan the vast scenes described here, with the ground falling away at one's feet, but I never experience the same thrill here as I do on Crib Goch. On the latter I have the impression of complete detachment, coupled with the prospect of a higher peak ahead which has still to be conquered and I look up. Here, however, on Yr Wyddfa, the peak has been won, the pendant ridges far away and I look down. Moreover, there is the constant reminder of other human beings, augmented during the summer season by the crowds that have not come up the hard way, and if you feel as I do, dear reader, walk over the Snowdon Horseshoe on a sunny day in early spring or late autumn when the profound solitude of this lofty ridge will act as a balm to your soul.

Plate 12 **Route 1** The Snowdon Horseshoe from Crib Goch

Moel Siabod

Pinnacles

Crib Goch

Lynnau Mymbyr

Llyn Cwmffynnon

To Snowdon and
Crib y Ddysgl

Plate 13 **Route 1** The Paths on Crib y Ddysgl

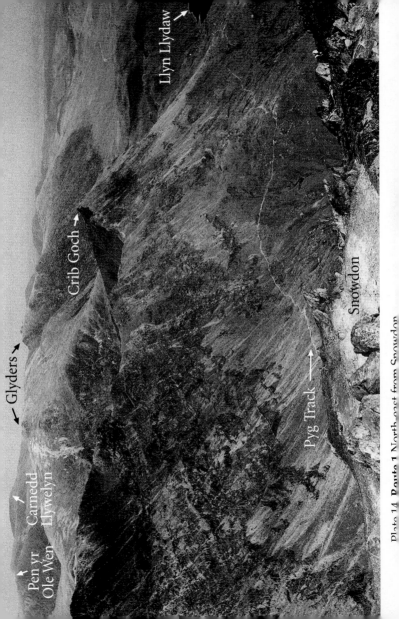

Pen yr
Ole Wen

Carnedd
Llywelyn

Glyders

Crib Goch

Llyn Llydaw

Pyg Track

Snowdon

Plate 14 **Route 1** North-east from Snowdon

Plate 15 **Route 1** South-east from Snowdon

Route 2. The Pyg Track. Follow Route 1 as far as Bwlch y Moch where the path forks and take the left branch which undulates slightly across the southern flanks of Crib Goch. It is well defined throughout and one of the most popular routes to Snowdon, and, moreover, it has the advantage of disclosing on the L one of the most dynamic views of the majestic cliffs of Lliwedd beyond Llyn Llydaw. Yr Wyddfa towers into the sky ahead until a prominent cairn is reached above Glaslyn and it reveals this blue lake below at the foot of its precipices. At this point the track goes to the R and is joined by the Miners' Track coming up from this lake, whence the steep ascent of the zigzags leads to the skyline at Bwlch Glas, where Route I is joined and followed to the summit of the reigning peak. A seven foot free standing monolith marks the point of emergence of this track on Bwlch Glas, and in descent will be a most useful indication of the exact point at which to leave the ridge, invaluable in snow, mist and bad weather.

Route 3. The Miners' Track. Leave the car park at Pen y Pass by the old road leading to the Copper Mines. It is a well cared for track and rises at a gentle gradient with views on L of Moel Siabod and the sylvan Vale of Gwynant. It contours round the south-eastern slopes of the *Last Nail in the Horseshoe*, and at a sharp turn to R reveals Lliwedd, Snowdon and Crib Goch towering ahead. The route now takes a direct line for the peaks and passes round and above Llyn Teyrn on L, whose shore is marked by derelict buildings, and thereafter bears R until Llyn Llydaw is reached. This is a superb viewpoint because it unveils one of the classic and most majestic prospects of Yr Wyddfa, while on L of it there is also a good view of Lliwedd. Keeping the lake on L, the broad track crosses its lower end by a causeway, which very occasionally is flooded and then necessitates a detour to the R. The path winds along the shore of Llyn Llydaw, passes some derelict mine buildings which are a legacy of the days when copper was mined in these hills, and

Plate 16 **Route 2**

Zig-Zags

Bwlch Glas

Snowdon

Plate 17. Routes 2 and 3 as and the Zig-Zags

← Lliwedd

Bwlch Glas →

Bwlch y Saethau →

Y Gribin →

Miners' Track →

Plate 18 **Route 3**—Snowdon from Llyn Llydaw

Llyn Llydaw

Causeway

Miners' Track

Bach   Lliwedd   East Peak   West Peak

Llyn Llydaw

Miners' track

Plate 20 **Route 3**

Snowdon

Miners' Track

then turns sharp R when the first considerable rise is encountered. The path mounts to the R of the stream coming down from Glaslyn, with Yr Wyddfa towering into the sky ahead, and later reaches the outflow of this sombre lake. Thence the level path rims its north shore, passes mine workings which should be avoided and more derelict buildings, until an eroded steep scree track on R rises to join the Pyg Track, where Route 2 is followed to the summit of Snowdon.

Route 4. Lliwedd and Bwlch y Saethau. Follow Route 3 to Llyn Llydaw and bear L on reaching the lake. The track rises gently at first, but do not take the rather indistinct branch on the R at the fork because this is used by rock climbers making for the cliffs of Lliwedd. After this the path deteriorates and becomes very rough as it rises steeply to the Col between Gallt y Wenallt on the L and Lliwedd Bach on the R. There is a prominent cairn on the ridge that is a useful landmark in mist. Now turn south-west and keep to the crest of the ridge, with sensational drops on the R, first over the lesser eminence of Lliwedd Bach and thereafter over the East Peak of Lliwedd, where the precipices on the R disappear into space, with Llyn Llydaw far below. There is a slight fall to the little Col ahead and then a rise to the West Peak of Lliwedd, where the grand retrospect is worthy of attention as it is one of the most dramatic scenes on the Horseshoe. Still keeping to the edge of the cliffs, the well-marked track descends over tricky rock and boulders, and care is needed here as a slip on the R would be fatal. The path levels out on the approach to Bwlch y Saethau and is joined by the Watkin Path coming up on the L from Cwm Llan. The last section, rising diagonally over scree to Yr Wyddfa, is the most trying part of this ascent, and while this most used track slants to the L across the shattered flanks of the peak to join the Rhyd Ddu path above Bwlch Main, some people may prefer to make a direct attack upon it and emerge on the skyline on the east shoulder of Snowdon below the

Snowdon

Glaslyn

Plate 22 **Route 3**

Zig–Zags

Pyg Track

Miners' Track

Miners' Track

Glaslyn

Plate 23 **Routes 2 and 3**

Bwlch y Saethau

Gribin Ridge

Lliwedd

Glaslyn

Plate 34 This scene is an oblique... of Plate 33...

To Snowdon →

West
East
Peaks of Lliwedd

Llyn Llydaw

Bach

Plate 25 **Route 4**

Lliwedd East Peak

Plate 26. Return ascent of Route 1 from the West Peak.

cairn. This is not recommended as a line of descent owing to exposure and causing considerable erosion.

Route 5. The Watkin Path. This popular ascent leaves the main road threading Nant Gwynant opposite the car park at Pont Bethania GR 627506. A cattlegrid gives access to the road leading to Hafod y Llan farm, but after some 500 metres it bears L through the rhododendrons along the old miners' road and emerges above the stream coming down from Cwm Llan. A charming waterfall is passed on the R and above it an almost level stretch passes some derelict mine buildings on R, goes over a wooden bridge to Plas Cwm-Llan GR 621521 also on R, and with a view high up on the L of the summit of Yr Aran. This one-time pleasant residence was used during the Second World War as a target for Commandos and is now an unsightly ruin. From here the track passes close to the Gladstone Rock on L, where a tablet commemorates the opening of this path by Gladstone then eighty-four years of age, on September 13th 1892. The yawning mouth of Cwm Llan now opens up ahead and is entered by a shaly path leading to a deserted slate quarry but turn sharp R before reaching the roofless buildings and climb steadily with Bwlch Main towering on L and Craig Ddu rising on R. A little rock gateway appears on the skyline ahead and this reveals the most shattered front of Snowdon, from where the path meanders round to the R and ultimately joins Route 4 on the crest of Bwlch y Saethau. The view from this pass comes as a surprise; for it discloses Glaslyn below and the full length of Llyn Llydaw beyond to the R, between which a rough rock spur, known as Y Gribin, affords a greasy and exposed scramble for those wishing to reach Route 3.

Route 6. Yr Aran and Bwlch Main. Follow Route 5 to Plas Cwm Llan but just before reaching it take the grassy path on the L which rises gently to cross the old mine railway line,

Plate 27 **Route 5**—A waterfall beside the Watkin Path

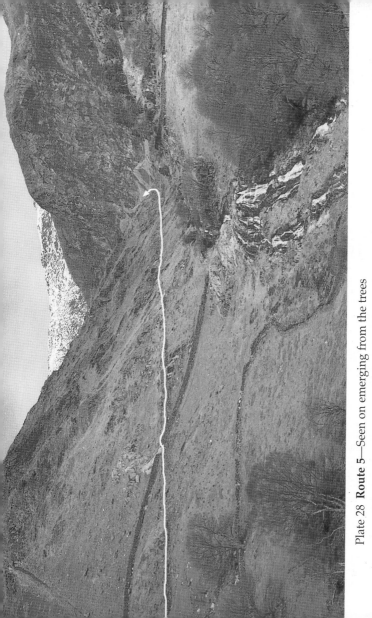

Plate 28 **Route 5**—Seen on emerging from the trees

Plate 30 **Routes 5 and 6**

SEF ODDIAR Y GRAIG HON I'R MAE'R CHORUS
SY GWR A WDD DDERBIO W.E. GLADSTONE A.S.
PAN ... WELE VENYDD ... DDIWEDDARAF A MEISON WYD YDD OED

DROFODD EIFRI AP
IAWNDER I GYMRU

CANODD Y DYRFA EVYWNAU CYMRU
A HEN WLAD FY NHADAU

SEP 13th 1892 — UPON THIS ROCK
THE RIGHT HONOURABLE W.E. GLADSTONE M.P.
WHEN PRIME MINISTER FOR THE FOURTH TIME AND 83 YEARS OLD
ADDRESSED THE PEOPLE OF EIFION UPON
JUSTICE TO WALES

THE MULTITUDE SANG CYMRIC THIS
AND "THE LAND OF MY FATHERS"

PUBLICLY DEDICATED BY SIR EDWARD AND LADY WATKIN JUNE 1993

Plate 32　The terminal stretches of **Route 5**

Yr Aran

bends L and R at an easy gradient and passes a derelict mine building on L before rising towards old mine workings on L GR 615516 (keep clear of these as the excavations are deep). From this point, scramble up the grassy bank to the ridge where you turn R and follow a dry stone wall along its crest, crossing it before the steepest section of the path rises to the summit cairn; it opens up splendid prospects in all directions; with a fine vista to the north-west of Mynydd Mawr and Llyn Cwellyn, and a grand view slightly north of east, of Moel Siabod with a glimpse of Llyn Gwynant below. But the magnificent perspective of the South Ridge of Snowdon will rivet the gaze and its crest affords the final section of this route to Yr Wyddfa. There is at first, a sharp descent to Bwlch Cwm Llan, where a rock-bound pool on the R and an almost round little tarn on the L will charm the eye. Thereafter the collar work begins: keep to the edge of the sharp drops on R and on attaining the saddle the Rhyd Ddu Path comes in on the L from Llechog, GR 605537 and from here ascend the clearly marked track along Bwlch Main to attain the cairn on the summit of the peak.

Route 7. Rhyd Ddu and Llechog. This easy ascent is one of the neglected delights of the group and incidentally most rewarding to photographers. There are two starting points: that nearest Beddgelert is preferable for those without a car and the other, just outside the hamlet of Rhyd Ddu, is preferred by motorists because South Snowdon Station, GR 571525, on the long-disused Welsh Highland Railway, has become a spacious car park and is quite close to the gate giving access to the main route. The key to the former is Pitt's Head GR 576515 on the Beddgelert Caernarfon road. Turn R here for the sequestered farm of Ffridd Uchaf, easily recognised by its embowering shield of conifers; pass it on L and follow the grassy track until it merges with the quarry road coming up from Rhyd Ddu. The key to the latter is an iron gate from which the disused

Plate 34 **Route 6**

Craig Cwm Silyn Nantlle Hills Y Garn II

Llyn y Gadair

Plate 35 **Route 6**—South-west from Yr Aran

Foel Goch

Mynydd Mawr

Craig y Bera

Llyn Cwellyn

Plate 26. Bryn-y-... West from Yr Aran

Moel Siabod

Llyn Gwynant

Cwm Llan

Yr Aran

Plate 37 **Route 6**—North-east from Yr Aran

Snowdon

Plate 28. Bwlch Main. Final stretch of **Routes 6 and 7** – note train and hotel

quarry road goes due east. Pass a deep quarry on R, conspicuous by the V-shaped opening in its far wall, and follow the
road as it contours round the hillside until some bold rocks
are encountered on L. This is a splendid viewpoint for the
appraisal of Llyn Cwellyn, enclosed on L by Mynydd Mawr
and on R by Foel Goch. A few steps ahead pass through
another gate and circle the crag opposite for the next turn in
the track which otherwise might be missed. There is an iron
gate on L situated at the point of mergence with the Beddgelert
track. Walkers who are familiar with this route could vary it
by continuing along the old quarry road past the iron gate with
fine views ahead of Yr Aran. This leads to the old South
Snowdon mine buildings from where Bwlch Cwm Llan
GR 605522 can be easily reached and Route 6 followed to the
summit of Snowdon. Our route now takes a direct line for
Llechog, well seen on the skyline with Yr Wyddfa on R, and it
winds its way uphill in and out of rocky outcrops, eventually
to reach another gate in a substantial stone wall, with a large
sheepfold on the other side. This is a good near-viewpoint for
Yr Aran, and also for the many tops of the Moel Hebog range
in the distant south-west. The path is unmistakable and soon
crosses a level green clearing containing the ruin of a hut, long
ago used as a place of refreshment, after which it rises more
steeply over rock and scree ultimately to thread the boulders
scattered in profusion on the broad crest of Llechog. This is a
revealing coign of vantage, since its steep slabs fall into the
vast basin of Cwm Clogwyn, embellished by several twinkling
tarns, and on R to the conspicuous shoulder and serrated ridge
of Bwlch Main. Farther to the R there is a grand array of the
peaks crowning the Moel Hebog group, below which Llyn y
Gadair and Llyn Cwellyn reflect the afternoon light. Now
climb the broad stony track to the saddle and here join Route 6
for the summit of Snowdon, meanwhile enjoying the enchanting views on R of Cwm-Llan and of Moel Siabod above Bwlch
y Saethau.

Pitt's Head

Moel Hebog

Photo 39. *Key to Route 7*

Plate 40 Start of **Route 7** for walkers from Beddgelert

Snowdon →

Rhyd Ddu Path →

Plate 41. Early stage of **Route 7** from Rhyd Ddu

Plate 42 **Route 7**

Saddle

Snowdon

Llechog

Ffriod Uchaf

Rhyd Ddu

Moel Eilio →

Crag y Bera →

Track to Snowdon

Cwm Clogwyn →

Elechog

Plate 44 Retrospect from **Route 7**

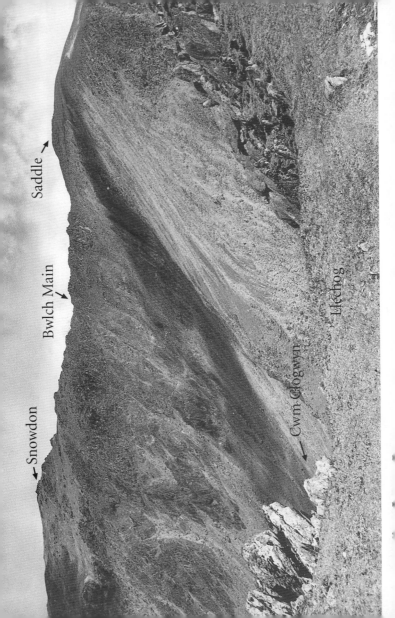

Snowdon ←

Bwlch Main ↓

Saddle ←

Cwm Clogwyn →

Llechog

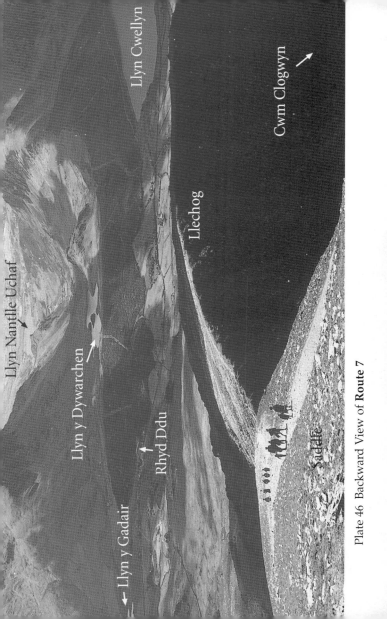

Plate 46 Backward View of **Route 7**

Snowdon Ranger Hostel

Snowdon Ranger

Route 8. The Snowdon Ranger. This could well be the oldest route to Snowdon and is named after its first guide who may have lived in or near the present Youth Hostel which faces the rippling waters of Llyn Cwellyn. It yields a very pleasant approach to Yr Wyddfa and is seldom crowded, save on those rare occasions of public holidays when it is invaded in force. Leave your car in the park opposite GR 564551 and start the ascent by crossing a stile to the L of the Hostel and make for the farm farther up the green hillside. Then zigzag through the pastures above it and go through a gate in a stone wall. This gives access to a wide grassy path, with a wonderful retrospect of Mynydd Mawr and Llyn Cwellyn, and farther on of the Nantlle Ridge and Moel Hebog. Go through a small iron gate and then tread the gradually rising moorland path, with a grand prospect ahead of Cwm Clogwyn, enclosed on L by the slopes of Clogwyn Du'r Arddu, on the R by the cliffs of Llechog, and dominated by Yr Wyddfa.

The well-trodden path passes below Bwlch Cwm Brwynog, but walk up to it on L and rest awhile to enjoy the fine retrospect of the Moel Hebog range on the other side of the valley behind you. Then, instead of rejoining the path on R, keep carefully to the crest of Clogwyn Du'r Arddu, and from a safe viewpoint look down its beetling precipices, which are the playground of the expert rock climber, to the stygian waters of Llyn Du'r Arddu, cradled in a wilderness of boulders at the foot of the crags. From the top of this eminence note the view of the Snowdon Railway near Clogwyn Station, backed by the shapely tops of the Glyders. Thereafter, return to the track on R and follow it to the summit of Snowdon, of which the section below the fork comes up from Llanberis.

Note – An alternative approach starts at Bron Fedw Isaf GR 568546 and is waymarked to join the original track higher up the hillside.

Mynydd Mawr

Craig Cwmbychan

Llyn Cwellyn

Youth Hostel

Nantlle Ridge ← Y Garn II

Llyn Cwellyn

Plate 49 View R of **Route 8**

Moel Hebog   Moel yr Ogof   Moel Lefn

Llyn y Gadair

Clogwyn Du'r Arddu   Snowdon   Cwm Clogwyn   Llechog

Plate 51 **Route 8**

Snowdon

Clogwyn Du'r
Arddu →

Llyn Padarn and Llanberis

Llyn Du'r Arddu

Clogwyn Du'r Arddu

Plate 53 Bird's-eye view of Llyn Du'r Arddu from **Route 8**

Snowdon

Carnedd Ugain

Route 9. The Llanberis Path. This is the longest, least arduous and most popular route to Snowdon, it involves a walk of about eight kilometres over a gently graded path. The key to this route is the square at the end of the first side road above the Snowdon Railway Station, where a gate gives access to a mountain by-road, with the railway on R GR 584597. Walk along the road to Cader Ellyll GR 582588 and turn L, the path continues to rise, passes under the railway, and then levels out right up to the Halfway House. The majestic cliffs of Clogwyn Du'r Arddu are now revealed and they appear on R until the path rises above them after passing Clogwyn Station. Hereabouts is the real reward of the ascent; for by going over to the spur nearby, the most dramatic view is obtained of the Llanberis Pass, far below and hemmed in by the steep slopes of Snowdon and the Glyders. Continuing the ascent, the path goes under the railway and keeps beside it and below the dome of Crib y Ddysgl all the way to the end of the line, whence the large cairn just above the cafe crowning Yr Wyddfa is quickly attained.

Warning. Although Route 9 is the easiest ascent of Snowdon, winter conditions can transform it into one of the most dangerous. For in deep snow the path disappears and walkers tend to keep to the railway or what can be seen of it. The most dangerous section is between Clogwyn Station and Bwlch Glas, where a shelf which carries the line fills up with snow that lasts much of the winter. It becomes hard and icy and very difficult to traverse safely. And since several fatal accidents have occurred here all walkers should pay particular heed.

Route 10. Cwm Glas. This sporting route is seldom used, save by the connoisseur who can revel in the solitude and wild grandeur of Cwm Glas, which is decked with Alpine flora in the spring and graced by a lovely tarn that opens up a surprising view of the Glyders. Follow Route 1 to the shallow

Snowdon

Crib y Ddysgl

Crib Goch

Llanberis Pass

Esgair Felen

Plate 56 **Railway and Route 9** run side by side

Moel Siabod

Glyder Fawr

Llanberis Path →

Snowdon Railway →

Llanberis Pass ↗

Clogwyn Station

Plate 58 **Route 9**

valley after the jumbled boulders GR 641554 and then bear R over a grassy shoulder to a small knoll GR 636556 that is the only sure key to the path. The path goes below Craig Fach and is cairned but rather indistinct in places, contours round the slopes below Bwlch y Moch, and then ascends over stony ground to a cairn perched on the northern spur of Crib Goch, above Dinas Mot GR 624560. The Cwm is now revealed ahead and is enclosed by mural precipices in which the Parson's Nose, a prominent cliff popular with rock climbers, is centrally situated. The path skirts the western flanks of the spur and then continues along a grassy shelf, to end where the stream falls from Llyn Glas. A short step uphill brings it into view. This is a remote and delightful spot in which to soliloquise on a warm sunny day; for the rocky shelf holding the lake in its grip cuts off all sound of traffic in Llanberis Pass below, and the only sign of life is the occasional person wending their way across the lofty ridge of Crib Goch on the southern wall of the Cwm. There are two exits from here: the first and easiest and most amenable is to walk up beside the stream feeding the tarn in the direction of the Pinnacles, and then to climb the scree on R to Bwlch Coch; from here continue along route 1 over Crib y Ddysgl and Garnedd Ugain. The second option is to go R of the Parson's Nose, pass a tiny lake cupped in bare rock, Llyn Bach. From this lake take a long diagonal ascending line out R to the ridge leading to Gyrn Las GR 612558 and pick a route carefully among the shattered rocks and slippery vegetation. On attaining the ridge you will arrive a little way above Clogwyn station on route 9 and that route is followed to the summit.

This second option out of Cwm Glas is not at all pleasant and in winter conditions presents a formidable undertaking only to be attempted by those with experience and training in the use of ice axe and crampons. The gully directly at the back of the corrie is known as Parsley Fern and is a Grade 1–2 winter climb often sporting a large and sometimes unstable cornice.

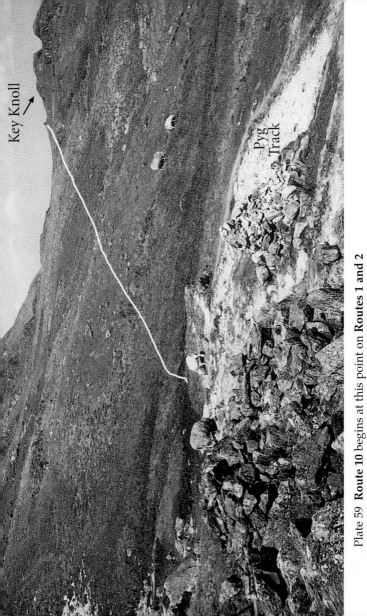

Key Knoll

Pyg Track

Plate 59 **Route 10** begins at this point on **Routes 1 and 2**

Northern Spur of Crib Goch

Dinas Mot

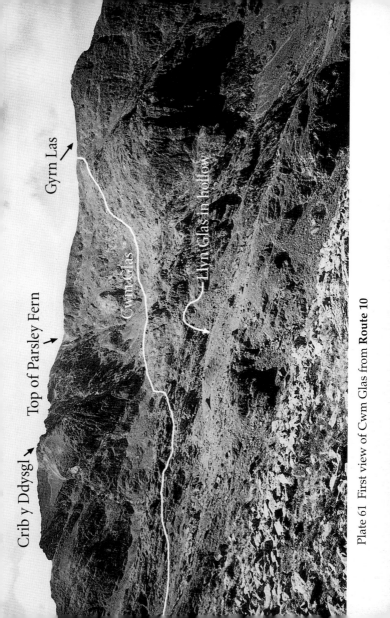

Crib y Ddysgl

Top of Parsley Fern

Gyrn Las

Cwm Glas

Llyn Glas in hollow

Plate 61 First view of Cwm Glas from **Route 10**

Crib Goch

Pinnacles   Bwlch Coch

Camping Site

Llyn Glas

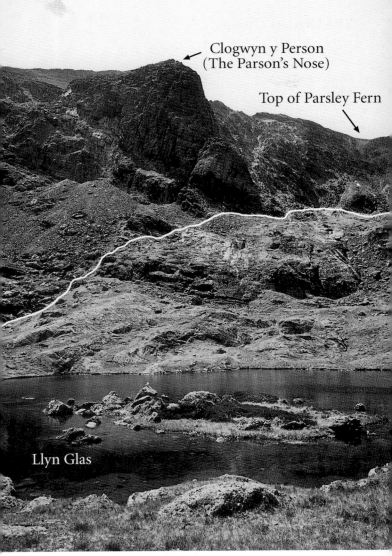

Clogwyn y Person
(The Parson's Nose)

Top of Parsley Fern

Llyn Glas

Plate 63 **Route 10**—Second exit

The Glyders Group

Glyder Fawr	999 metres	3277 feet
Glyder Fach	994 metres	3261 feet
Y Garn	947 metres	3106 feet
Elidir Fawr	924 metres	3031 feet
Tryfan	915 metres	3002 feet
Foel Goch	831 metres	2726 feet
Carnedd y Filiast	821 metres	2693 feet
Mynydd Perfedd	812 metres	2664 feet
Nameless Peak	805 metres	2641 feet
Bwlch Caseg Fraith	788 metres	2588 feet
Elidir Fach	782 metres	2564 feet
Esgair Felen	762 metres	2500 feet
Gallt yr Ogof	763 metres	2503 feet
Bwlch Tryfan	716 metres	2350 feet

OS Map: Landranger 115 Snowdonia
Outdoor Leisure 17 Snowdon & Conwy Valley

When seen from the south and west, the range of hills dominated by Glyder Fawr looks comparatively uninteresting as it
merely displays a succession of vast grassy slopes interspersed
here and there with outcropping rocks that are crowned by the
sharp little top of the Castle of the Winds. The only notable
exception is that of the single spur of Esgair Felen, whose
reddish broken cliffs catch the eye and overhang the craggy
declivities confined to this one point on this side of the group,
bordered by the Llanberis Pass.

But when seen from the north this aspect changes dramati-
cally and comes as a complete surprise; for one savage cwm
follows another from east to west, all of them hemmed in by
striking mural precipices. The range is further enhanced by the

beautiful isolated peak of Tryfan, and amid the whole stands Ogwen Cottage, the hub of the many ascents from this side of the group. Moreover, the summit ridge of the Glyders is unique in Wales and characterised by a grand display of chaotically arranged boulders whose desolate aspect vies with that of the main ridge of the Cuillins, in the Misty Isle of Skye, for pride of place in wild Britain.

In view of these remarkable features it is not to be wondered at that the range draws legions of walkers, and there are so many routes up and over the group that many days can be spent in their exploration. All the important ascents are dealt with in the following pages, any or all of which may be ascended by persons in fit and vigorous condition. In snow, even on a clear day, climbing in the Glyders requires the utmost care when ice axe and crampon experience is absolutely essential.

Glyder Fawr
Route 11. Ogwen Cottage and the Devil's Kitchen. There are a number of car parks in the valley, all are well placed for ascents of the routes described. The main parking areas are below the Milestone Buttress, another half way to Ogwen Cottage and a commodious third between the Cottage and Youth Hostel. GR 649604. It is here that our route begins, and later on keeps well above the marshy ground eventually to turn sharp R for Llyn Idwal. On arriving at the lake there is a double stile over the boundary fence of the Cwm Idwal National Nature Reserve, which opens up a revealing view of the first section of the route ahead, with the great cleft of the Devil's Kitchen on the skyline. Keep the lake R, pass Idwal Slabs L, and ascend the well-marked path which bears R and eventually threads the immense boulders below the Kitchen. The retrospect from the mouth of the cavern is magnificent, with Llyn Idwal below, Llyn Ogwen in the middle distance and the Carneddau in the background, dominated by the

Maes
Caradoc

Ffridd-Trwgwn

1044m

Cae

Braich-du

Mynydd
Perfedd

Craig-ddu

Bwlch-y-
Brecan

Centre

Llyn
Ogwen

Foel
Goch

Llyn Cwion

Falls

Pont Pen-y-benglog

303m

23m

831m

Fawr

YH

25

11

13

16

Cwm Clyd

Y Garn

26

916m

15

Tryf

26

Hwal

Llyn
Bochlwyn

24a

Nant
Natur
Tm
Devils Kitchen

12

937

Llyn-y-Cwn

beris

14

Llanberis

Afon Las

99

Glyder

24

Esgair

Llyn

999m

Clyder Fawr

2

A 4086

Pass

of

Llanberis

Llyn Cwn
Ffynnon

23

22

Pont-y-Gromlech

GWYN

356m

Y Fael
Berfedd

Pen
Notel

Cwm Glas

Llyn Glas

Crib Goch

Pen-y-Pass
Nature Trail

Bwlch
Gwy del

65m

921m

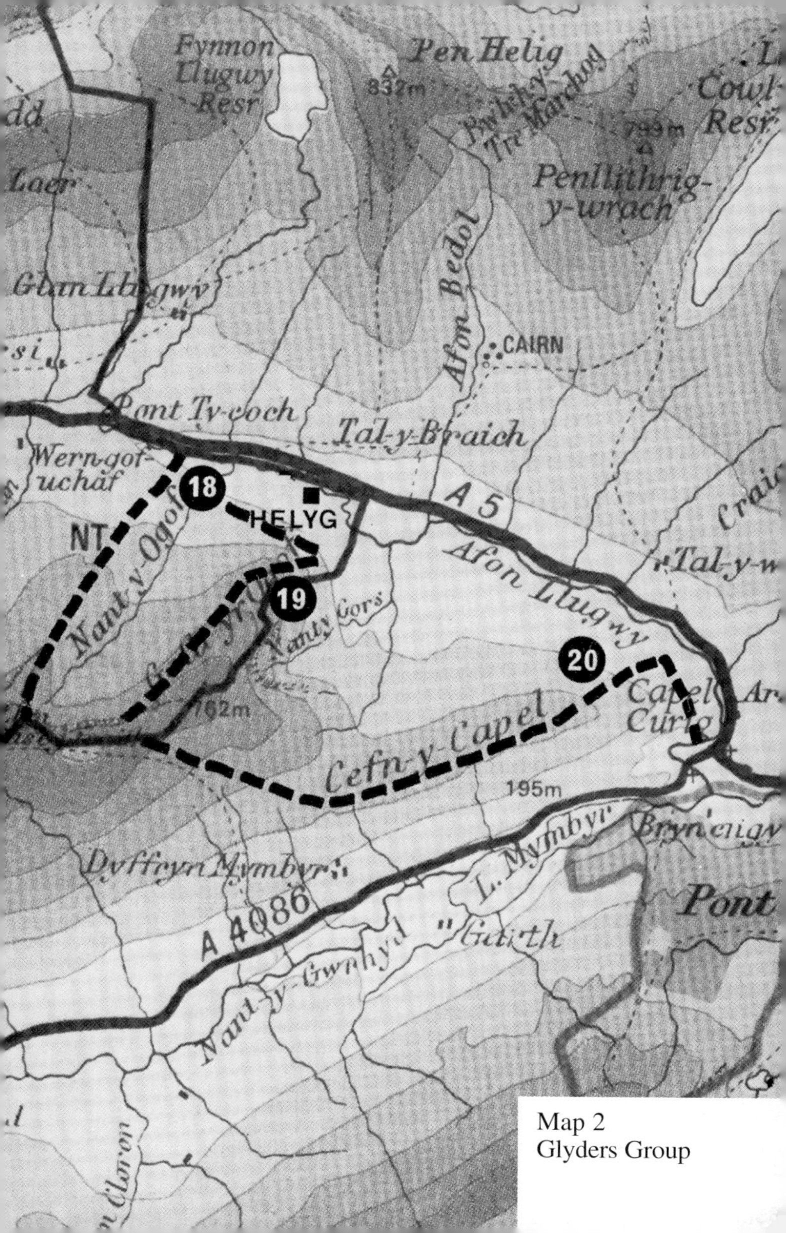

Map 2
Glyders Group

shattered front of Pen y Ole Wen. Now turn L and climb the steep, boulder-strewn shelf to the skyline where a prominent cairn marks the route. Continue ahead towards Llyn y Cwn R, GS 6358, and then L to mount the twisting scree path which ultimately emerges on the broad summit of Glyder Fawr. This is one of the most desolate spots in Snowdonia, and a peculiarly spike-shaped eminence dominates this rocky top of the highest peak of the group.

The panorama from this stony wilderness is extensive, but restricted by the plateau-like top of the mountain. The view to the east along its wide ridge may first catch the eye, since its forlorn aspect suggests what might well be the surface of the moon. The Castle of the Winds GR 654582 appears below the great heap of stones that characterise Glyder Fach, about a kilometre and a half distant, on L of which rises the summit of Tryfan. To the south Snowdon and Crib Goch present a serrated skyline, and to the west Mynydd Mawr tops the ridge enclosing the Llanberis Pass, while to the north the vast bulk of the Carneddau stretches away in the distance, crowned by the prominent summits of Carnedds Dafydd and Llywelyn. This coign of vantage stands at the head of four valleys, but to see them on a clear day involves a stroll round the rim of the plateau. They are: Nant Ffrancon to the Menai Straits; the Conwy Valley to the sea near the Great Orme; Nant Gwynant to Harlech and the sea and Llanberis Pass to Caernarfon.

When this Route is used for the descent to Ogwen, it is a worthwhile detour to pick up the stream from Llyn y Cwn and to follow it to the top of the Devil's Kitchen, see plate 102. To regain the path it is preferable to retrace your steps to the lake.

Route 12. Cwm Idwal and the Nameless Cwm. Follow Route 11 to Idwal Slabs, but bear L up the grassy slopes before reaching them. When the Nameless Cwm opens up R, ascend the ridge above Idwal Slabs to the skyline, from where you head due south-west up to the cairns on Glyder Fawr. This is

Plate 65 **Route 11**—Idwal Slabs

Devil's Kitchen

Idwal Slabs

Llyn Idwal

Plate 66 **Route 11**

Glyder Fawr

Nameless Cwm

Llyn y Cwn

Devils Kitchen
(the way down)

Pen yr Helgi-du

Penllithrig-y-wrach

Tryfan

Creigiau Gleision

Glyder Fach

Castle of the Winds

Plate 68 Eastern prospect from Glyder Fawr

Nameless Cwm

Idwal Slabs →

Llyn Idwal

known as The Seniors Ridge and can present some interesting and difficult scrambling propositions by its most direct ascent.

Route 13. The Gribin. Leave Ogwen Cottage by Route 11, and on arriving at the first sharp turn to the right continue straight, along the path to Llyn Bochlwyd. On arriving in the Cwm turn R along the lower grassy slopes of the Gribin. GR 651592. On attaining the crest of the Gribin, Tryfan and Llyn Bochlwyd are seen to the east, where the blue of the lake, surrounded by its green carpet of grass, contrasts strongly with the pale stony declivities of the mountain. The ridge rises gently at first over grass, with glimpses R of the Devil's Kitchen and Y Garn, and eventually changes abruptly to rock. Climb carefully until its top GR 650583 is attained and you will see ahead and slightly L the disintegrated slabs of the Castle of the Winds, which fall precipitously into the cwm. Turn R on the ridge, pass the forlorn hollow of the Nameless Cwm R, and follow the path through the stones and strange collections of crags to the summit of Glyder Fawr.

Nameless Cwm

Y Gribin

Castle of
The Winds

Glyder Fach

Bristly Ridge

Bwlch
Tryfan

Bwlch Tryfan

Llyn Bochlwyd

Plate 71 **Routes 14 and 15** Seen from The Gribin

Y Gribin · Y Garn · Elidir Fawr · Carnedd y Filiast

Bristly Ridge →   ← Glyder Fach   ← Castle of The Winds

Plate 73 **Route 13** Top of the Gribin

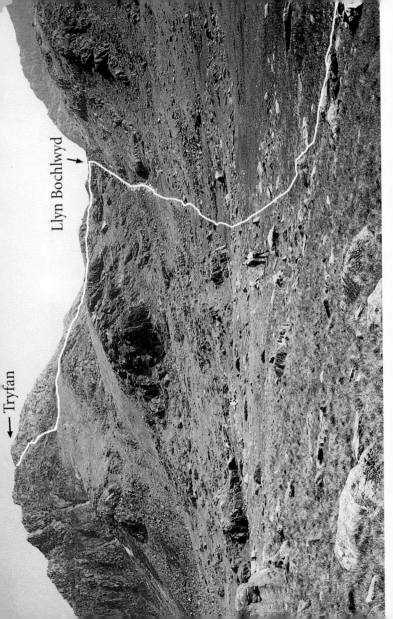

← Tryfan

Llyn Bochlwyd

Route 14. Llyn Bochlwyd, Bristly Ridge and Glyder Fach.
Follow Route 13 to the stream coming down from Llyn
Bochlwyd. Climb beside it until this sombre lake comes into
view and rest awhile by its shore to contemplate its wild
situation. It is enclosed L by Tryfan and R by the Gribin, while
ahead rise the cliffs supporting Glyder Fach which are a
favourite playground for the rock climber. Proceed by keeping
the lake R and tread the gradually rising path which bears L
by this wedge-shaped mountain to arrive at Bwlch Tryfan
GR 661587. Go over the stone wall by a stile and turn R where
the route to the Bristly ridge is plainly visible since it bears the
scratchmarks of thousands of people who have passed this
way. On reaching the base of the crags the track rises steeply
and twists in and out of buttress and pinnacle. Most of the
difficulties can be overcome by turning them on the right but
those with a steady head will find little difficulty in keeping a
more direct ascent. You emerge finally on a broad stony ridge.
Now turn south-west and go over to inspect the Cantilever L,
a great slab poised securely on vertical crags, whose top may
be reached by an easy scramble. Then continue ahead to Glyder
Fach R whose massive pile of boulders is a conspicuous
landmark hereabouts. Scramble to the top if you feel like it,
but be careful, and then go over to the Castle of the Winds.
Beyond is a fine prospect of Snowdon and a view of the
gradually rising plateau ending at Glyder Fawr. It is better to
climb straight over the Castle rather than take the circuitous
course L round its base, and descend carefully through the
maze of vertical slabs on its far side. Walk down to the Col and
there join Route 13 for the summit of the reigning peak of the
group.

Plate 75 **Route 14**—Llyn Bochlwyd

Carnedd Llywelyn

Tryfan

Pen yr Helgi-du

Bristly Ridge

Plate 76 Retrospect from **Route 14**

Plate 78 **Route 14**—Glyder Fach

Crib Goch

Snowdon

Crib y Ddysgl

Castell y Gwnt

Glyder Fawr

Top of Y Gribin

Route 15. Ogwen Cottage and Tryfan Scree Gully. Follow Route 14 to Llyn Bochlwyd. Turn L at the lake and ascend grassy slopes until directly below the conspicuous scree gully that emerges to the L of the summit of Tryfan. This arduous route is difficult, with many loose boulders.

Route 16. The North Ridge of Tryfan. This is one of the most interesting and entertaining scrambles in all Wales and the usual starting point is near the head of Llyn Ogwen, but the lower shoulder of the mountain may also be reached by a direct ascent from the other side of the ridge. Go through a gate L of the Milestone Buttress GR 664603 and climb the long twisting staircase that first mounts beside a wall R and later in the shadow of the Buttress itself. Below the buttress turn L and eventually the track emerges on the shoulder which is covered with deep heather and has a cairn marking the meeting of several paths GR 667599; it might even be called the Piccadilly Circus of Tryfan for tracks radiate and rise sharply up the North Ridge. The alternative approach from the east comes in here, and it is the point of departure for Heather Terrace which rises diagonally across the eastern flanks of the peak below its three prominent buttresses. This landmark may be avoided by walkers who do not object to the ascent of a long scree slope, for one goes up from the bend in the track some 200m below this cairn. From this point there are so many variations in the route to the next shoulder that it is a matter of personal taste as to which of them is chosen, but that centrally situated can be most easily followed. Many parts of it are steep and slippery, and there are a few tricky bits where a conveniently placed handhold assists the passage. It rises diagonally R round speculative corners and past the "Cannon", a huge leaning rock that is well seen from Ogwen, until eventually the second shoulder is attained. This platform calls for a halt, if only to scan the horizon which has widened enormously as height was gained. At this stage perhaps the most striking prospect is that

Cairn

To Milestone Buttress

This stile no longer exists

Plate 80 The lower reaches of **Route 16**. The stile no longer exis

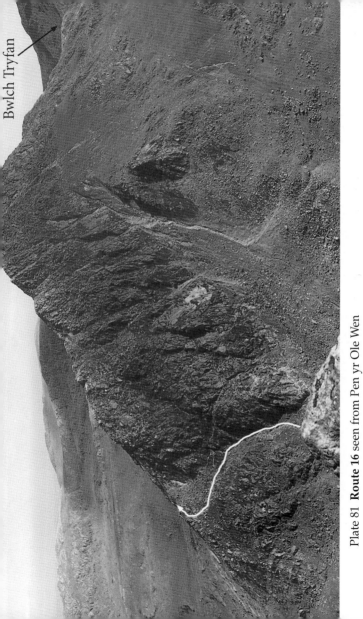

Bwlch Tryfan

Plate 81 **Route 16** seen from Pen yr Ole Wen

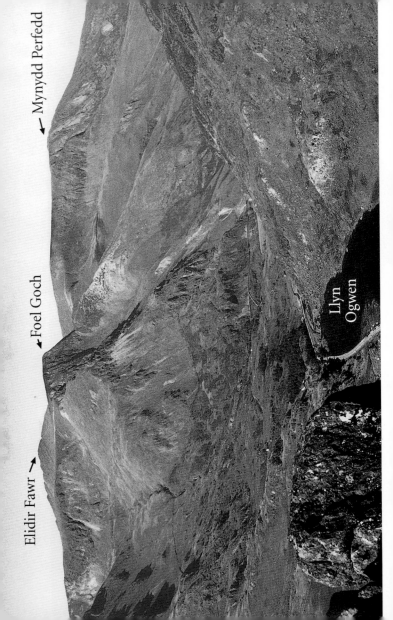

Mynydd Perfedd →

Foel Goch →

Elidir Fawr →

Llyn Ogwen

of Llyn Ogwen, now far below, which even on sunny days looks bleak and forbidding against its brightly coloured engirdling hill slopes.

Ahead rises the last obstacle in this sporting course and since it consists entirely of rock it is best to tackle it direct from the point where the track ends against the cliff. However, there is an alternative L, where a faint path leads eventually into the North Gully which is jammed with boulders and slabs to afford an enclosed variation to the other more exposed route. Both routes merge at the Col between the North Peak and the summit and it is only a short step to Adam and Eve, the two conspicuous upturned boulders that crown the summit of Tryfan.

On a sunny day it is usual to find a number of fellow enthusiasts gathered round this lofty perch: for it is a pleasant spot on which to eat lunch, to tackle the spectacular and risky "step" from Adam to Eve and to enjoy the spacious panorama. The vista R and L along the valley extending from Capel Curig to Bethesda is of course attractive and divided by Llyn Ogwen far below. It is bounded on the north by the vast green slopes of the Carneddau whose broad ridges culminate in Carnedd Llywelyn. But their smooth flanks do not attract the eye so strongly as the immediate landscape of the Glyders themselves, where Llyn Idwal and Llyn Bochlwyd sparkle on the floor of the rockbound cwms stretching westwards. Bristly Ridge forms a broken wedge to the south, and the eye wanders R over the ridge to the crags supporting the Gribin, passing centrally the very tip of Snowdon which will be missed even on a clear day by those who do not possess an alert and discerning eye! Farther R the skyline rises gently to Glyder Fawr, and then after a fall to the Devil's Kitchen rises again to Y Garn and continues westwards in an almost flat line to Foel Goch above which the curving ridge of Elidir Fawr will draw the eye. It then passes over Mynydd Perfedd, finally to merge with the rising slopes of Pen yr Ole Wen.

There is still a long way to go to Glyder Fawr and in consequence you must not linger too long on this airy seat; so begin the descent by crossing the crest that leads to the South Peak and glance back at the summit of Tryfan to grasp more clearly its isolated situation. Then carefully descend the twisting track which passes in and out of gaps between the boulders and eventually reaches a little Col separating the main peak from its shapely satellite, on top of which L lies a charming rock-bound pool reflecting the colour of the sky. GR 664592, Spotheight 830. Now bear R and wander down the clearly marked path to Bwlch Tryfan, there to join Route 14 to the crowning peak of the group.

Y Garn

Elidir Fawr →

Foel Goch →

Route 17. Heather Terrace. If you come by car, park it at the farmhouse of Gwern-y-Gof-Uchaf, GR 674605, which stands back from the road L just above the head of Llyn Ogwen. Heather Terrace is clearly revealed as a diagonal line rising across the face of Tryfan. Leave the back of the farm and pass L some inclined slabs which are used as a practice ground by rock climbers. Then join the path R which crosses some marshy ground and later rises over scree to the cairn noted in Route 16. Now proceed L in and out of a collection of boulders that stand amid thick heather and bilberries to gain the Terrace, which is followed upwards past the base of the three buttresses and their adjacent gullies, all of which rise into the sky right up to the summit of Tryfan and afford one of the most treasured playgrounds of the rock climber. At the termination of the Terrace ascend R and go over a low stone wall to the col, at which point join Route 16, near the rock pool described in the descent to Bwlch Tryfan, for the remainder of the ascent.

Route 18. Bwlch Caseg-ffraith. The ridge rising to this pass from the Ogwen Valley is one of the most revealing and least used in this group of hills. It is a paradise for the photographer, and as long ago as 1941 I gave an account of it in my *Snowdonia through the Lens,* when a friend came with me from Helyg to Pen y Pass over the Glyders in superb Alpine like conditions. Yet, although I have since ascended it on several occasions I have never encountered another walker or photographer with whom I could share the rare beauty of the magnificent scenes it unfolds.

The key to this route is the farmhouse of Gwern-y-Gof-Isaf, GR 685601, which nestles at the very root of the ridge on the south side of the Afon Llugwy, almost opposite Helyg. Those who come by car may park their vehicle near the farm. The ridge rises in grassy steps, interspersed with crags which become more plentiful as height is gained; it is enclosed R by Cwm Tryfan and L by Nant yr Ogof. About half-way along its

crest there is a grand prospect of Tryfan across the cwm, and from this height the peak assumes its true elevation and under snow assumes the splendour of an Alpine giant. The ridge steepens and later flattens out on a lofty plateau rimmed with crags, on which repose Llyn Caseg-fraith, GR 670583, and two smaller pools. They are priceless gems in a sombre setting and on a calm day reflect the upper buttresses of Tryfan to perfection. There is also a splendid view of Bristly Ridge L, whose pinnacles and buttresses are clearly delineated by the sunlight before noon. A rather indistinct track threads the soft marshy ground hereabouts, and on leaving the platform it crosses the Miners' Track which comes up from Pen y Gwryd and over to Bwlch Tryfan beneath the crags of Bristly Ridge. Thereafter our route skirts the rim of Cwm Tryfan and eventually joins Route 14 at the top of Bristly Ridge.

Route 19. Gallt yr Ogof. This rounded craggy eminence is the first of the Glyder group to come into view L when proceeding westwards along the Holyhead road from Capel Curig. It may be reached conveniently by walking along the old road from this village where a car may be parked. But a nearer approach for those arriving by car is to park at the farm as for Route 18. At the farm turn L to walk a short distance along the old road to the base of the mountain, whence a nice scramble up a conspicuous diagonal gully places you on the skyline. Here you turn L for the summit and then bear R for the Nameless Peak whose far side slopes down to Llyn Caseg-fraith. At the lake you join Route 18 for the ascent to Glyder Fawr.

Plate 86 **Route 18**—Buttresses of Tryfan. Heather Terrace is plainly obvious. **Route 17**

Tryfan

Bristly Ridge

Plate 87 Starting point of **Route 18**

Miners' Track to Ogwen →

Plate 89 Bristly Ridge seen from **Route 18**

Plate 91 **Route 19**—Gallt yr Ogof from the Holyhead Road

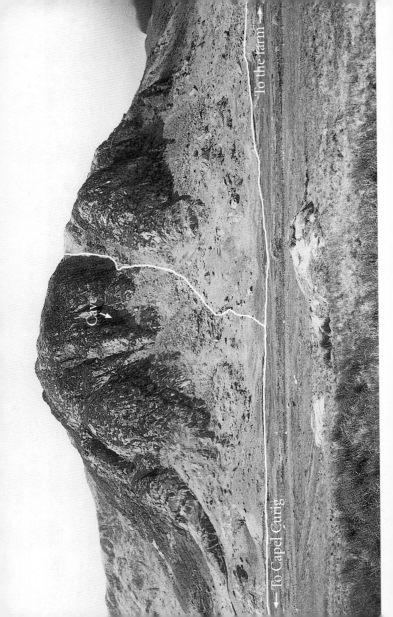

Route 20. The Ridge from Capel Curig. The long and lofty ridge of this group begins almost at the very doors of the village and its complete traverse, followed by the descent from Glyder Fawr to Ogwen Cottage, requires good weather and a long day. The best approach to it is by the lane L of the Post Office and General Store in Capel Curig. Parking is available just across the bridge over the noisy cataract of the Afon Llugwy. Follow the old Ogwen road to the derelict barn beyond the last cottage whence bear L along the rising path until the higher ground is attained. If a direct line along its crest is taken several craggy eminencies will be encountered, and it may be desirable to turn them on L or R. In due course pass round the rim of Nant y Gors R and make for the Nameless Peak to join Route 19 for the remainder of the long tramp.

Car park

Route 21. Pen y Gwryd and the Miners' Track. This popular path begins at a stile below the hotel GR 661558 and at a bend in the road opposite Llyn Lockwood. It takes a more or less direct line for the end of a stone wall running uphill R, which is reached after crossing the stream coming down over bare slabs from Llyn Cwmffynnon. The ground hereabouts is very boggy and even when walking beside the wall several very wet patches are encountered. These terminate on passing through a gap in the wall, near a sharp corner L. Thence a cairned track slants uphill R through rock and heather, and at the end of this steep section it is worthwhile to look back at the fine vista down the Vale of Gwynant, and R to the Snowdon Horseshoe. Now continue the ascent at an easier gradient, past a waterfall L until a break in the rock ridge overhead gives access to vast areas of marshy ground on the summit plateau. Go forward until Llyn Caseg-fraith appears ahead. Here join Route 18 to Glyder Fawr L, or if proceeding to Ogwen Cottage follow the well-marked track that contours round the head of Cwm Tryfan, below the crags of Bristly Ridge to Bwlch Tryfan and the reverse of Route 14.

Plate 94 Vale of Gwynant from **Route 21**

Plate 95 The Glyders from Pen y Gwyrd

Route 22. Pen y Gwryd and Llyn Cwmffynnon. This is the most direct route from the south to the reigning peak of the group. Cross the stile below Pen y Gwryd and walk uphill L to reach the outflow of the lake. Continue R round its shore and on reaching the stream, entering it from the Glyders, walk by its banks and take the L branch which rises through the wide opening of Heather Gully. The going is very rough but not as steep as it looks from afar, and the route terminates quite suddenly by the cairns on Glyder Fawr. If the main stream is followed it will lead to the col below the Castle of the Winds, but by bearing L on reaching the grassy slopes the summit of Glyder Fawr may be attained.

Route 23. Pen y Pass and Esgair Felen. Walk round the western end of the Youth Hostel GR 647556 and cross the wall by a stile. Ascend the well marked stony track and on reaching the skyline it opens up a comprehensive view of Llyn Cwmffynnon and the Glyders. Turn L up the long grassy shoulder of Glyder Fawr, past a remarkably perched boulder L, and when near the top of the slope bear L for the conspicuous red precipitous crags of Esgair Felen. This is a magnificent coign of vantage for the appraisal of the Crib Goch – Crib y Ddysgl section of the Horseshoe, for the view into Cwm Glas opposite with the stream falling steeply to the pass below, and for the long vista down the Llanberis Pass to the twin lakes at Llanberis. Having savoured this wonderful panorama turn around and ascend the broad ridge northeastwards that terminates on the summit of Glyder Fawr.

← Glyder Fawr

← Castell y Gwynt

Llyn Cwmffynon

Plate 98 **Route 23** Llanberis Pass from Esgair Felen

Glyder Fawr →

Dinas y Gromlech →

Esgair Felen →

Route 24. Nant Peris and Llyn y Cwn. Motorists may park in a large car park in Nant Peris GR 607584 for the start of this fine walk. Go to the bus stop at Gwastadnant in the Llanberis Pass GR 614576 which is about a kilometre above the church in Nant Peris, and there turn L along the stony walled path. This passes a traditional stone cottage and then goes through a small gate beside a larger one to follow the wall on the L towards a second cottage. Here a wooden stile gives access to a waymarked path which crosses a field to the Afon Las. Now turn R and ascend the steep true L bank of the stream and higher up cross a second stile. Keep to the wall running uphill for some 60–70 metres, then take a diagonal course to the R where the eroded track appears ahead. Keep to the R of the cascading stream and also the waterfall on the skyline, whence the gradient becomes easier and is well cairned through Cwm Cneifio where boggy ground leads straight to Llyn y Cwn. Here turn R and ascend the final stages of Route 11 to Glyder Fawr.

If you are bound for Ogwen Cottage by the latter route, it is worthwhile to first bear L beyond the tarn and pick up the stream that leads to the Devil's Kitchen, GR 637587 and there observe the striking view of Llyn Idwal and Llyn Ogwen through the vertical walls of the chasm (Plate 102). Do not attempt to descend the Kitchen which is the strict preserve of the properly equipped rock climber.

It is essential that all walkers adhere strictly to this route as it was closed some time ago before being reopened and waymarked by the National Park warden service.

Plate 101 **Route 24** passes R of the waterfall

Carneddau

Llyn Ogwen

Llyn Idwal

Plate 102 **Route 24** Looking down the Devil's Kitchen

Elidir Fawr.
This peak is one of the more westerly of the Glyders group and presents a fine wedge shaped elevation when seen from Carnedd Llywelyn. It is often climbed from Ogwen by way of Y Garn when the distance to be covered is almost 16 kilometres, whereas if ascended from Nant Peris it is considerably less. This approach has received some attention by the Warden Service, due to the popularity of Elidir Fawr as one of the fourteen peaks, of which details are as follows:

Route 24a. Nant Peris and Elidir Fawr. Park all vehicles in the main car park at Nant Peris GR 607584 and walk into the village, turn R just beyond the Vaenol Arms pub by a chapel and follow the tarmaced road which rises gently round to the L to a gate. Pass through it and continue along the cart track leading to Fron Farm GR 605590, but just before reaching a second gate, near a small cottage, break over a field to the R up to a wall and the stile set over it. A stone barn appears ahead and the path goes through a gate on its R and then begins to zigzag over grass to gain height. Around the 350 metre contour it bears L and takes a gently rising line into Cwm Dudodyn on the R which is a public right of way. But on reaching an iron footbridge over the chattering Afon Dudodyn you cross it and the real collar work begins. It is a stiff climb all the way to the summit of Elidir Fawr, and to facilitate the crossing of a high mountain wall higher up its grassy slopes stiles have been erected . This lofty coign of vantage opens up a wide panorama round the western arc, and includes Anglesey and unusual prospects of the Snowdon Range.

Elidir Fawr

Plate 104 **Route 24a**—Retrospect from the zig-zags: Fron Farm on the R

Y Garn and Foel Goch
Route 25. Ogwen Cottage and Llyn Clyd. These two mountains make a picturesque backdrop to the western prospect from the head of Llyn Ogwen, and when seen by morning light a dark shadow is cast into the wild cwm immediately below the summit of Y Garn, in which repose, out of sight from this viewpoint, the small tarn of Llyn Clyd and a placid pool just above it. The direct ascent of this peak is tough and unyielding, and there are two well-defined tracks: the fishermen's route is if anything less steep and rises to the L of the stream to end at Llyn Clyd; the other route is some distance R and takes a direct line to the grassy ridge hemming in the cwm.

Follow Route 11 to Llyn Idwal and bear R along its shore, crossing the bridge over the stream that flows from the lake. Pass round a boggy hollow and then ascend one or other of the alternative tracks already mentioned. Keep to the well-trodden path which rises along the crest of the north-east ridge all the way to the cairn on Y Garn, and meanwhile note the wild prospect of the cwm below L. The isolated summit of Y Garn is a grand viewpoint and to the south unfolds a grim prospect of Snowdon and its satellites, with R views of Llanberis and the sea on a clear day. But it is the Glyders themselves that will hold the gaze, for their rocky cwms are disclosed to perfection across the void. Tryfan and Llyn Ogwen will catch the eye to the east and the riven declivities of Pen yr Ole Wen on the other side of Nant Ffrancon to the north contrast strangely with the smooth green slopes of the Carneddau in the background. Now walk in a north-westerly direction and keep to the rim of the cwm R all the way to Foel Goch, whose cairn is scarcely as revealing as that of Y Garn. This tramp, together with the return descent, is enough for the average pedestrian's day, but strong walkers should continue along the lofty ridge to Mynydd Perfedd which opens up a striking prospect of Elidir Fawr L, with Marchlyn Mawr below. Those bound for Llanberis may traverse Elidir and descend to Nant Peris by reversing Route 24a.

However, those who wish to shorten their route may descend direct to the Nant Peris valley from Foel Goch by way of Esgair y Ceunant to the south-west, where a stile has been erected over the high mountain wall.

Route 26. Ogwen Cottage and the Devil's Kitchen. Follow Route 25 to the boggy hollow and pick up the track L that skirts Llyn Idwal with splendid views of Idwal Slabs L. Then continue its ascent through the boulders to the Kitchen, and bear L to climb the shelf which emerges on the Llyn y Cwn plateau – as for Route 11. Here turn R and scale the grassy slopes of Y Garn, making sure you keep to the marked path to avoid further erosion, and on encountering craggy ground on the edge of the ridge, glance down to Llyn Clyd before attaining the cairn on the summit of this peak.

Llyn Clyd

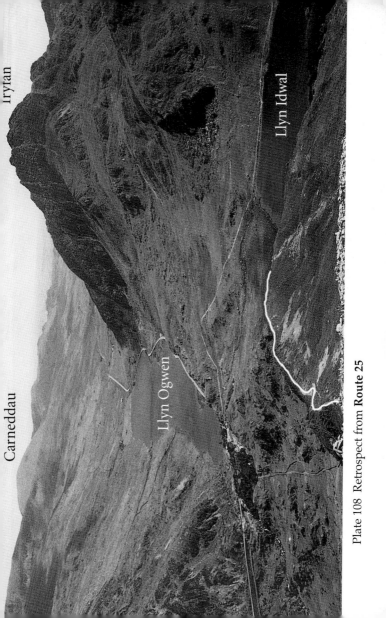

Iryfan

Carneddau

Llyn Ogwen

Llyn Idwal

Plate 108 Retrospect from **Route 25**

Lliwedd

Crib Goch

Esgair Felen

Cwm Glas

Snowdon

Crib y Ddysgl

Clogwyn Du'r Arddu

Glyder Fawr

Nameless Cwm

Castle of The Winds

Glyder Fach

Bristly Ridge

Y Gribin

Llyn y cwn

Plate 110 **Route 25**—The Glyders from Y Garn

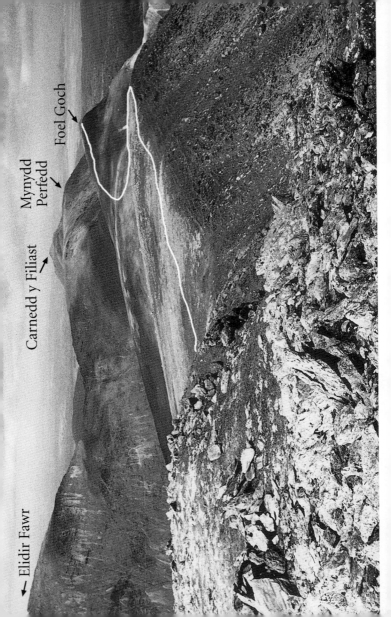

Elidir Fawr

Carnedd y Filiast

Mynydd Perfedd

Foel Goch

Llyn Idwal

Plate 112 **Route 26**

Plate 113 Idwal Slabs from **Route 26**

The Carneddau

Carnedd Llywelyn	1064 metres	3490 feet
Carnedd Dafydd	1044 metres	3426 feet
Pen yr Ole Wen	978 metres	3208 feet
Foel Grach	976 metres	3202 feet
Craig Llugwy	970 metres	3184 feet
Yr Elen	962 metres	3156 feet
Foel Fras	942 metres	3091 feet
Yr Aryg	866 metres	2875 feet
Llwytmor	838 metres	2749 feet
Pen yr Helgi-du	833 metres	2732 feet
Pen Llithrig y Wrach	799 metres	2621 feet
Drum	770 metres	2526 feet
Craig Eigiau	735 metres	2411 feet
Creigiau Gleision	678 metres	2224 feet
Pen y Castell	620 metres	2034 feet
Tal y Fan	610 metres	2001 feet
Crimpiau	457 metres	1500 feet

OS Map: Landranger 115 Snowdonia
Outdoor Leisure 16 & 17 Snowdonia & Conwy Valley

The Carneddau comprise the largest group of hills in Snowdonia and consist mainly of broad grassy ridges, scantily interspersed with outcrops of rocks, save the well known cliffs of Craig yr Ysfa, Black Ladders and the steep shattered southern front of Pen yr Ole Wen.

They afford excellent walking country, free from major problems, but the distances to be covered in their exploration are misleading to the eye, and, moreover, the vast plateau-like summit of Carnedd Llywelyn is one of the mistiest spots in the group.

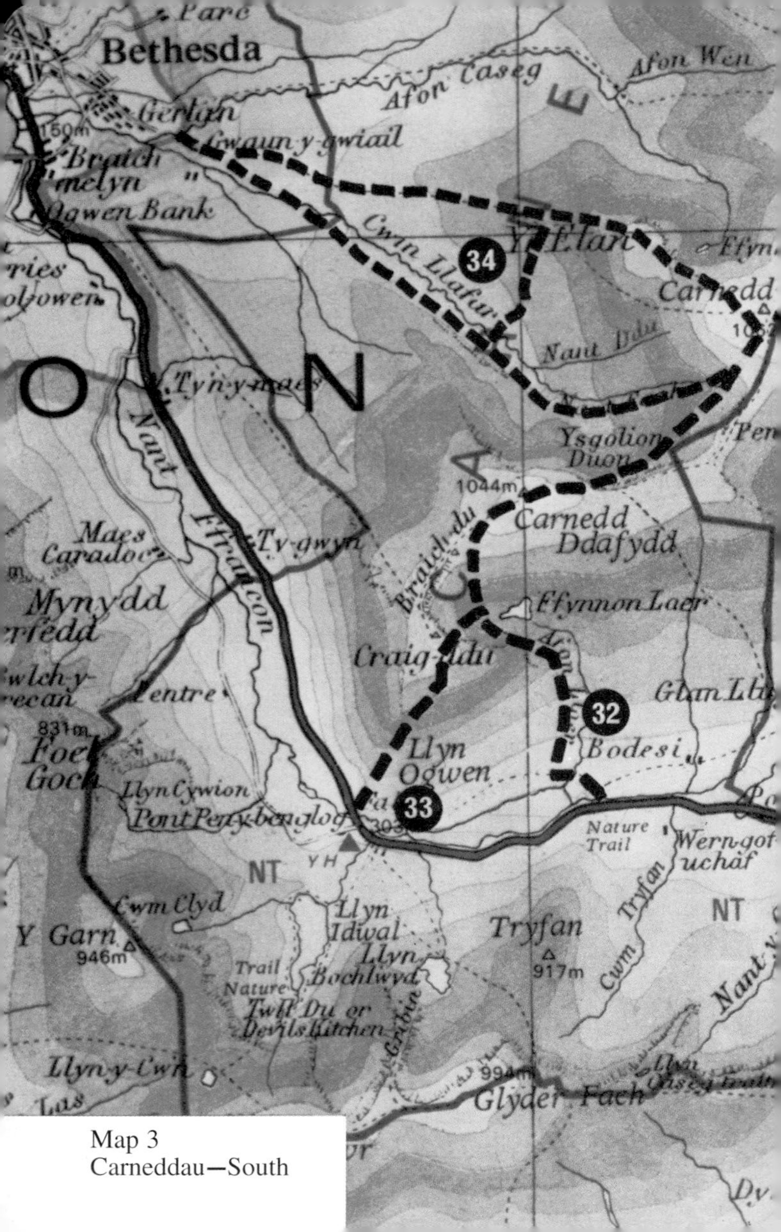

Map 3
Carneddau—South

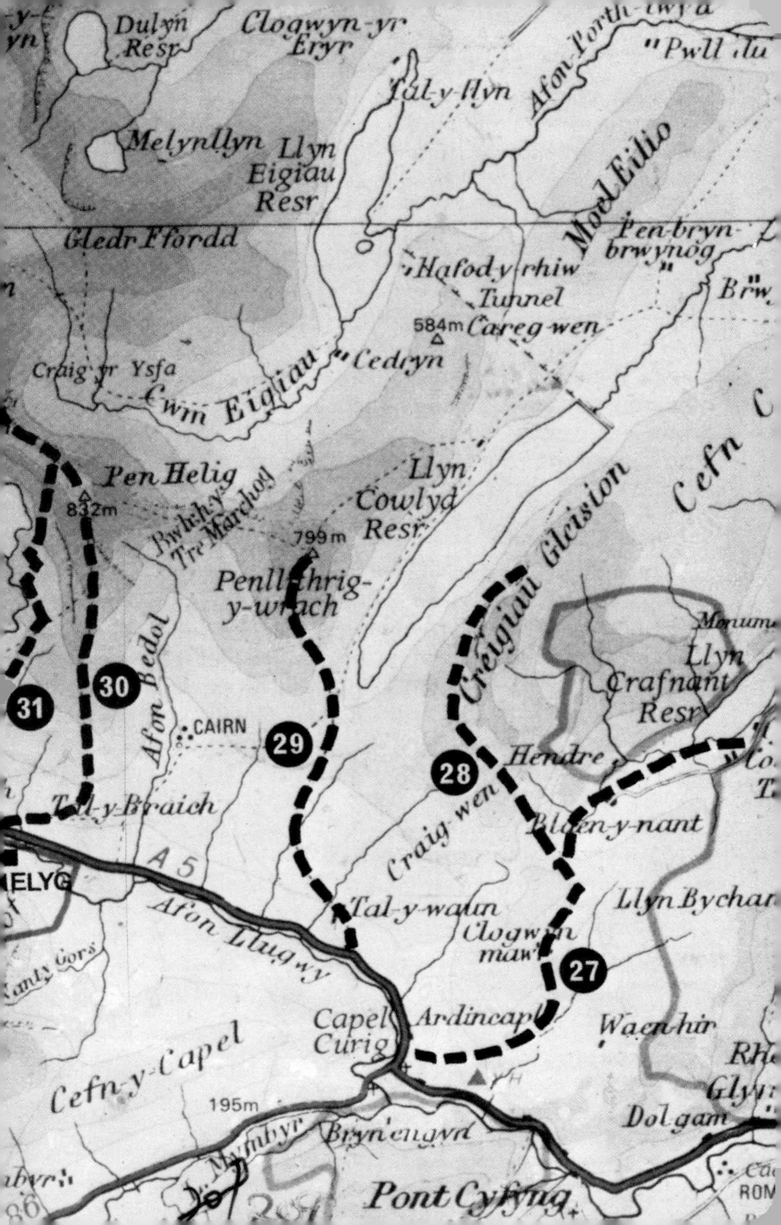

Dulyn Resr
Clogwyn-yr Eryr
Afon Porth-llwyd
Pwll du
Tal-y-llyn
Melynllyn
Llyn Eigiau Resr
Moel Eilio
Gledr Ffordd
Pen-bryn-brwynog
Hafod-y-rhiw
Tunnel
584m
Careg-wen
Craig yr Ysfa
Cedryn
Cwm Eigiau
Pen Helig
832m
Bwlch y Tri Marchog
Llyn Cowlyd Resr
799m
Penllythrig-y-wrach
Creigiau Gleision
Cefn
Llyn Crafnant Resr
31
30
29
28
27
Afon Bedol
CAIRN
Hendre
Tal-y-Braich
Craig-wen
Blaen-y-nant
A5
Afon Llugwy
Tal-y-waun
Clogwyn mawr
Llyn Bychan
Capel Curig
Ardincaple
Waen-hir
Cefn-y-Capel
YH
195m
Dolgam
Mymbyr
Bryn-engan
Pont Cyfyng

In extremely bad conditions walkers may go on to the small stone shelter some fifty to seventy five metres north east of the nearby Foel Grach summit GR 688659. Moreover, in this immense area it is easy to get lost in bad weather, and I therefore advise all to descend by one or other of the routes described herein if they wish to reach the valley safely.

The enormous whale-back ridges, though in places well cairned, can be difficult in mist owing to the absence of well defined landmarks, and in bad weather walks should be confined to the ascent of one or other of the peaks within easy reach of the Ogwen Valley. To make a successful traverse of the range in these conditions requires expert use of map and compass, together with long experience of the hills as a whole, but on clear days few difficulties should be encountered.

The following routes include most of the popular ascents, but in view of the vast distances from the well-known centres most of the northerly tops have been omitted from this work.

Unhappily, however, it will come as a great surprise and disappointment to all who are bound for Craig yr Ysfa when they find this cherished wilderness has been invaded by the Central Electricity Generating Board. For they have replaced the old straight track from Helyg which penetrated into the heart of the Carneddau with a road that ends at the dam constructed at Ffynnon Llugwy. The purpose of this 2.5 kilo-metre road is to service the reservoir which is part of the Dinorwic Pump Storage Scheme. This piece of vandalism in the Snowdonia National Park will always be an eyesore to every lover of this delectable part of Wales.

Route 27. Llyn Crafnant and Crimpiau. The easy walk to this lovely lake through a charming wild valley is one of the delights enjoyed by every visitor who stays in Capel Curig GS 7258 and if desired may include Llyn Geirionnydd GS 7660 on the return journey. However, the former may also be reached by car from Trefriw and the latter by turning off at the Ugly House. Hence, by combining walking with driving this enchanting corner of the Carneddau can be seen with the minimum of effort.

The route for pedestrians leaves Capel by the stile opposite the Post Office. Follow the path past the conspicuous Pinnacles R, then cross a stream where the ground is often damp, and go through another gate into some woods at the foot of a rocky eminence L. On emerging from the trees walk over the flat stones laid throughout in damp places, then cross another stream and continue uphill at an easy gradient until the valley comes into view ahead. Now pass round a vast stretch of marshy ground L and later bear R into the upper reaches of the valley which is hemmed in L by the craggy ridge that culminates in Crimpiau GR 733595. Continue ahead through rock and heather until the watershed is reached, whence pass through a wall and stroll downhill to the sylvan shore of Llyn Crafnant.

Crimpiau appears on the skyline L from the highest point of the path. GR 738595. Bear L here by a less distinct track and on reaching rougher ground keep R until a cairn is encountered in thick heather. Then zigzag more steeply through the scattered crags, taking whichever way is fancied, and eventually bear L to attain the little plateau whose summit cairn is conspicuous at its western end. The vista along the Ogwen Valley suddenly bursts upon the eye and will doubtless come as a great surprise. Looking round the great arc from L to R the panorama reveals: Moel Siabod and the Llynnau Mymbyr, Moel Hebog and part of the Snowdon Group, the immense mass of the Glyders, Tryfan, Foel Goch and the Carneddau from Pen yr Ole Wen to Creigiau Gleision. There is also a bird's-eye view of Llyn Crafnant.

Llyn Crafnant →

Capel Curig
CRAFT CENTRE

CELTIC CRAFTS

SPAR

capel curig post office
x e n a j ayron jones
self service grocers, off licence & delicatessen

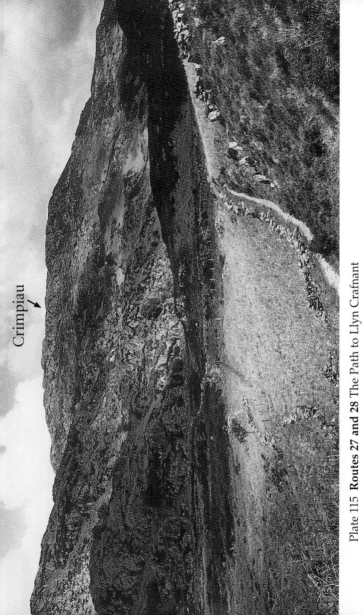

Crimpiau

Plate 115 **Routes 27 and 28** The Path to Llyn Crafnant

Llyn Crafnant

Path

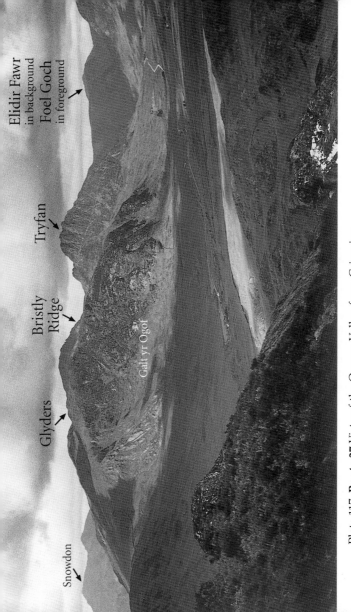

Elidir Fawr
in background
Foel Goch
in foreground

Tryfan

Bristly
Ridge

Galt yr Ogof

Glyders

Snowdon

Plate 117 **Route 27** Vista of the Ogwen Valley from Crimpiau

Route 28. Creigiau Gleision. This lofty ridge is nearly three miles due north of Capel Curig and the most easterly peak in the Carneddau over 600 metres in height. It is supported by a long line of broken crags, its crest is over a mile in length, and on the west its slopes fall steeply to Llyn Cowlyd. On the south east, however, its gradient is easier but dappled with crags, beneath which plantations of conifers descend to the shore of Llyn Crafnant.

Follow Route 27 to Crimpiau, pass the cairn and descend steep grass on its north side. Cross a wall at its highest point and pick up the track beyond it which leads to a large sheepfold GR 729599 immediately at the foot of Craig Wen, a prominent rocky eminence conspicuous in the view from Crimpiau. Continue along the now less distinct track keeping all craggy outcrops well R passing by Moel Defaid and Craiglwyn and on skirting the last of the knolls at spotheight 678m, the summit of Creigiau Gleision GR 733623 comes into view. The cairn stands on the highest section of the long ridge with steep drops to the northwest and opens up extensive views to the east, in which the blue of several tarns and lakes will catch the eye. To the west, however, views of the Carneddau are restricted by Pen Llithrig y Wrach on the other side of Llyn Cowlyd, but the south-western arc discloses Moel Siabod, the Glyders, Tryfan and Y Garn to advantage. Creigiau Gleision may also be reached by diverging R when Llyn Cowlyd comes into view during the ascent of Route 29.

Plate 118 Retrospect of **Route 28**

Creigiau Gleision

Plate 120 **Route 28**—The summit of Creigiau Gleison

Route 29. Pen Llithrig y Wrach. This pointed peak is the last sentinel on the ridge descending to the south-east from the dominating peak of the group, and is a conspicuous object when seen from Capel Curig. Park behind the post office GR 720581 and walk along the Holyhead road from the village and after passing Bron Heulog go through a narrow gate R and follow the track past Tal y Waun L. GR 717594. The direction across the moor was formerly indicated by some conspicuous power lines which have now been removed. In dry weather this was the most direct route, but as the terrain hereabouts is notoriously wet and boggy, it is better to bear L beyond the cottage, cross a low wall on the L of a deep pool and pick up a line of posts which later veer R to join the more direct route. A leat is eventually encountered, and although the more athletic walker may spring across it and land on a muddy bank, it is advisable to turn L until a bridge appears ahead. After crossing the bridge bear R over a stile, GR 717609, where the path opens up a fine prospect of Llyn Cowlyd below, enclosed by Pen Llithrig L and by Creigiau Gleision R. Now cross another plank L over a stream and make for a clearly marked grassy depression that terminates on the skyline, crossing several rocky outcrops en route. Then bear north over steep grass until the cairn surmounting Pen Llithrig appears on the skyline. The vast panorama round the south-western arc is revealing and includes all the familiar peaks from Moel Siabod to Carnedd Llywelyn, with below the latter a good view of Craig yr Ysfa R of the grassy Pen yr Helgi-du.

Plate 123 The view of Llyn Cowlyd from **Route 29**

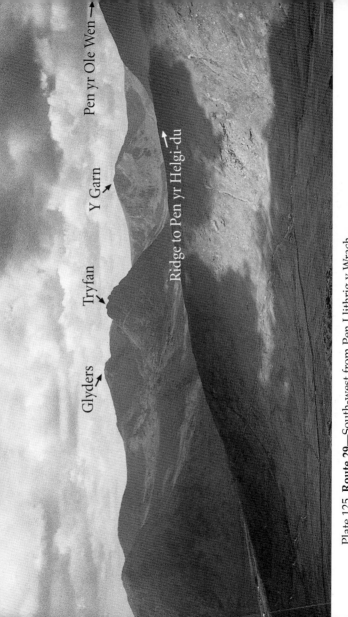

Glyders Tryfan Y Garn Pen yr Ole Wen →

Ridge to Pen yr Helgi-du

Plate 125 **Route 29**—South-west from Pen Llithrig y Wrach

Carnedd Llywelyn

Craig yr Ysfa

Pen yr Helgi-du

Carnedd Dafydd

Route 30. Pen yr Helgi-du. This is the culminating point of the grassy ridge that takes root at Tal y Braich, and its cairn is about 3 kilometres north of the Holyhead road. Parking is only possible at the farm of Gwern Gof Isaf GR 685601. It may be conveniently approached from Helyg, by taking the side road to Tal y Braich on the L of which is a conspicuous stile. Cross it and follow the grassy track to the north-west corner of the field where a bridge GR 700606 spans the leat which carries water from the hillside to Llyn Cowlyd R. Cross the bridge, and attain the lower slopes of the broad ridge, then keep to its gradually ascending crest until the cairn is reached, GR 698630. To the north it is steep and rocky, and those wishing to extend their walk may do so by crossing the narrow ridge to Craig yr Ysfa L, or by tramping over the broader ridge to Pen Llithrig y Wrach R. The spacious views unveiled from the summit are interesting and reveal Llyn Eigiau to the north, the hills about Capel Curig to the east, Gallt yr Ogof and the wedge of Tryfan to the south, and the precipitous crags of Craig yr Ysfa, crowned by the immense summit of Carnedd Llywelyn, to the north-west. By moving over to the edge of the summit plateau L, a bird's eye view is obtained of Ffynnon Llugwy, which occupies the floor of the wild cwm below. Those who ascend Pen yr Helgi-du *en route* for Carnedd Llywelyn may avoid the last rise to its summit by following a track L which provides an almost level course to the connecting ridge.

Route 31. Helyg, Craig yr Ysfa and Carnedd Llywelyn. This walk is one of the most interesting and revealing ascents in the Carneddau, and if the descent is made by reversing one or other of the following two routes it yields the finest circuit in this lofty group of hills, and moreover, is the most rewarding to the photographer. Park at Gwern y Gof Isaf and ascend the road that ends at Ffynnon Llugwy. At a derelict building on the R, go R on the track that rises gradually at first then steeply to Bwlch Eryl Farchog GR 635634. Here a carpet of heather and

Pen Llithrig y Wrach

Pen yr Helgi-du

Amphitheatre

Plate 128 **Route 30**—Craig yr Ysfa from Pen yr Helgi-du

Pen yr Ole Wen

bilberries makes a luscious foreground to the spacious view of Cwm Eigiau, with the blue of the lake shimmering in the distance and L, a prospect of the sharply falling crags of Craig yr Ysfa. The retrospect hereabouts is worthy of note, with Bristly Ridge and Tryfan, and Y Garn above Llyn Ogwen R. From the col climb a twisting path with a short scramble that emerges on the ridge above Craig yr Ysfa, Pen y Waen Wen GR 691638 but before going too far glance back at the route so far ascended with Ffynnon Llugwy below. Halt awhile on the rim of Craig yr Ysfa which discloses the vast Amphitheatre, hemmed in on either side by sheer cliffs that are the treasured playground of the rock climber. Note also the undulating ridge R which displays the sharp drops on the northern flanks of both Pen Llithrig y Wrach and Pen yr Helgi-du. Continue the walk by ascending the long ridge that terminates on the summit of the reigning peak of the group.

The top of Carnedd Llywelyn is a vast plateau, and is a place that requires care in mist owing to the difficulty in locating the safe ways off the peak. It supports a large cairn and its mossy surface is dappled with stones and strangely contorted groups of boulders. The panorama on a clear day is best seen by strolling round the rim of the plateau, and while it splendidly reveals the broad grassy ridges of this group trailing away to the north, with the shapely peak of Yr Elen L, it is the south-western arc that will hold the gaze. The Glyders, Snowdon and the top of Pen yr Ole Wen lead the eye R to the long ridge of Carnedd Dafydd, with a glimpse of the distant Rivals, Moel Elio and the beautiful sharp cone of Elidir Fawr, with still further R the sea stretching to infinity.

Ffynnon Llugwy

Plate 131 **Route 31**

Ffynnon Llugwy

Plate 133 **Route 31** Precipices of Craig yr Ysfa

Pen yr Helgi-du

Pen Llithrig y Wrach

Cwm Eigiau

Plate 135 The last ascent of **Route 31**

Yr Elen

Plate 137 **Route 31** View from summit

Route 32. Llyn Ogwen, Pen yr Ole Wen and Carnedd Dafydd.

Motorists may park along the side of the road or in one of the car parks along the shores of Llyn Ogwen. From the club hut of the Midland Association of Mountaineers at Glan Dena, GS 6660, take the track towards the farm of Tal y Llyn Ogwen, bear R before reaching the gate entrance to the farm and follow the wall for a short distance then cross the stile to get onto the path above which follows the Afon Lloer into the wide mouth of the wild cwm above. After climbing a stile in the wall turn L and make your way through the crags at the foot of the eastern spur of Pen yr Ole Wen, and above them ascend over grass and shale to the summit of this first peak. On the way, glance down into the cwm R and note the rough triangular shape of its lake. From Pen yr Ole Wen follow the well-worn stony track R whose ups and downs are clearly seen as far as the summit of Carnedd Dafydd. The summit is reached over a well scratched track across stones and boulders. Before departing this lofty peak, look back at the view whose skyline reveals the Glyders, Crib Goch and Snowdon above the enclosing slopes of Ffynnon Lloer, with the tops of Y Garn, Craig Cwm Silyn and Mynydd Mawr to the R. Now turn your steps in the direction of Carnedd Llywelyn, which appears as an uninteresting but massive, grassy hill. Descend L over the stones to a cairn and look down on the grim bastions of Black Ladders R, whose almost vertical cliffs are seldom visited except by winter ice climbers. Pass round their craggy rim by Craig Llugwy GR 678632 and make your way over the broad stony ridge to the summit of the highest peak of the group.

Pen yr Ole Wen

Ffynnon Lloer

Tal-y-llyn Ogwen

Llyn Ogwen

Plate 140 Cwm Lloer seen from **Route 32**

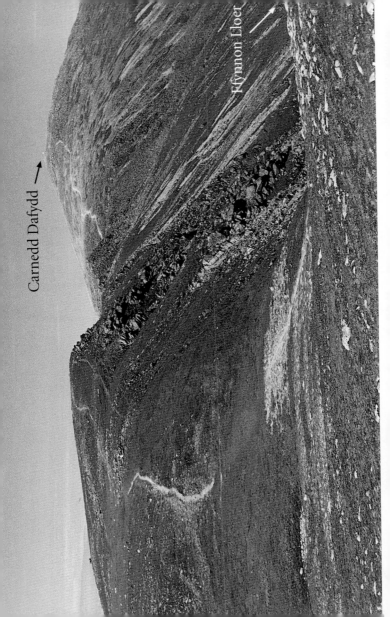

Carnedd Dafydd →

Ffynnon Lloer

Pen yr Ole Wen

Ffynnon Lloer

Plate 142 **Route 32**—Retrospect from Carnedd Dafydd

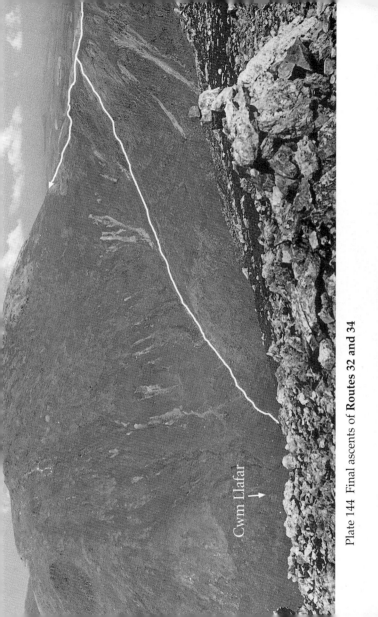

Cwm Llafar

Plate 144 Final ascents of **Routes 32 and 34**

Route 33. Ogwen Cottage and Pen yr Ole Wen. The direct ascent of this lofty sentinel is one of the toughest in all Snowdonia and should only be undertaken by those who revel in the ascent of slippery scree that is almost everywhere overgrown with deep heather.

Leave the Cottage GR 650603 and walk along the road towards Bethesda. Glance below the main bridge over the roaring waters of the river Ogwen and you will see the ancient packhorse bridge arched delicately above the torrent. Go over a simple stone stile set in the wall R and then over the rocks to gain the steep grassy slopes ahead, from where a narrow path winds its way aloft. On reaching a rough platform the real collar work begins, and although the ascent may be continued by any of the indistinct tracks through the heather, it is easier to bear R until the edge of the slope is reached and then zigzag L to the first top. Now climb over boulders to the second and real summit of the peak, beyond which you join Route 32 along the lip of Cwm Lloer and on to Carnedd Dafydd.

The view to the south from the ascent of Pen yr Ole Wen is one of the most striking in the region, because it not only discloses a remarkable prospect of the North Ridge of Tryfan, but also a superb vista right into Cwm Idwal far below. Glyder Fawr appears above Idwal Slabs, and Crib Goch, Snowdon and Crib y Ddysgl above the Devil's Kitchen. You should note that photographs of these dramatic scenes are best taken in the late afternoon of a clear summer day, when the westering sun illuminates the deep cwm to perfection by the elimination of too much shadow.

Plate 146 Tryfan and Llyn Ogwen from **Route 33**

Plate 147 **Route 33**—Cwm Idwal from the summit

Gwaun-y-gwiail

Route 34. Bethesda and Carnedd Llywelyn. This ascent begins with a long walk up a pleasant and spacious valley and concludes with a stiff climb at its head. In consequence the views are restricted until the peak is gained.

The route begins at Gwaun-y-Gwiail GR 638660 which stands at the broad mouth of Cwm Llafar. Parking can be very difficult to find and it may be preferable to park down in the village. You must not obstruct the lane. Follow the path with the Afon Llafar L and cross its tributary, the Afon Cenllusg, to continue beside the main stream. Ascend the path which mounts between it and the slopes of the steep ridge sur-mounted with crags R and with the grim cliffs of Black Ladders ahead. When Nant Ddu and Nant Fach join the Afon Llafar GR 665640 follow the latter to its source beneath Carnedd Llywelyn. Then climb straight up the steep grass to the ridge which is a broad col between Llywelyn and Craig Llugwy as for Route 32. From here bear north-east for the immense summit.

A longer variation takes in Yr Elen, which is reached by walking for about 2 kilometres along the path, when you should bear L up its western ridge over Foel Ganol GR 668655, and after passing the craggy summit of Yr Elen, keep to the narrow ridge, with steep drops L to the diminutive Ffynnon Caseg, until the crowning peak of the group is attained.

A third possibility is indicated in plate 149 where one ascends the long whaleback ridge of Carnedd Dafydd, passing Mynydd Du en route and taking care not to fall over the precipitous edge to the L. Once the top of Dafydd is reached continue as for Routes 32 and 33.

Carnedd Dafydd

Black Ladders

Cwm Llafar

Yr Elen

Plate 150 Starting point of **Route 35**

Plate 151 **Route 35**—Aber Falls

Plate 152 **Route 35**—The stream below the falls

Route 35. Aber Falls and Carnedd Llywelyn. This long walk is often undertaken by visitors staying as far away as Capel Curig, and the only convenient way of doing it is to persuade someone to drive you to Aber in the morning and to pick you up at an agreed spot in the Ogwen Valley in the late afternoon. The usual starting point is Pont Newydd, GR 663720, where there is ample parking. The path goes through a gate R of the bridge and is clearly marked as it winds its way beneath abundant trees for about two kilometres. It ends immediately opposite Aber Falls, where the Afon Goch takes a dramatic leap over some 60 metres of cliff. When the stream is in spate this splendid display should on no account be missed. This section of the valley is Coedydd Aber National Nature Reserve. The track to Carnedd Llywelyn bears L about 500 metres short of the fall and rises gradually across a vast scree slope. It then takes an exposed course on rocky slopes L, with sensational drops R to the base of the falls, and thereafter mounts over grass beside the musical cascades of the stream R. After passing a prominent sheepfold GR 671696 the valley widens considerably, with the craggy top of Llwytmor L, and Bera Mawr R, crowned with immense crags. The stream is followed as far as its sources between Foel Fras L and Yr Aryg R GR 680673. Now bear R across a marshy track and climb the latter peak, and from here follow the broad grassy ridge south-east first to Garnedd Uchaf then south over Foel Grach GR 689659 to Carnedd Llywelyn, with views R of the craggy ridge of Yr Elen below which nestles the tiny tarn of Ffynnon Caseg. Strong walkers may vary this route by leaving the Afon Goch at the sheepfold and ascending over grass to the rocky summit of Bera Mawr, GR 674682, then keep to the rising contours west of Yr Aryg and after crossing the spur of Foel Grach circle round Cwm Caseg and scramble up to the lofty connecting ridge of Yr Elen, which is visited before attaining Carnedd Llywelyn.

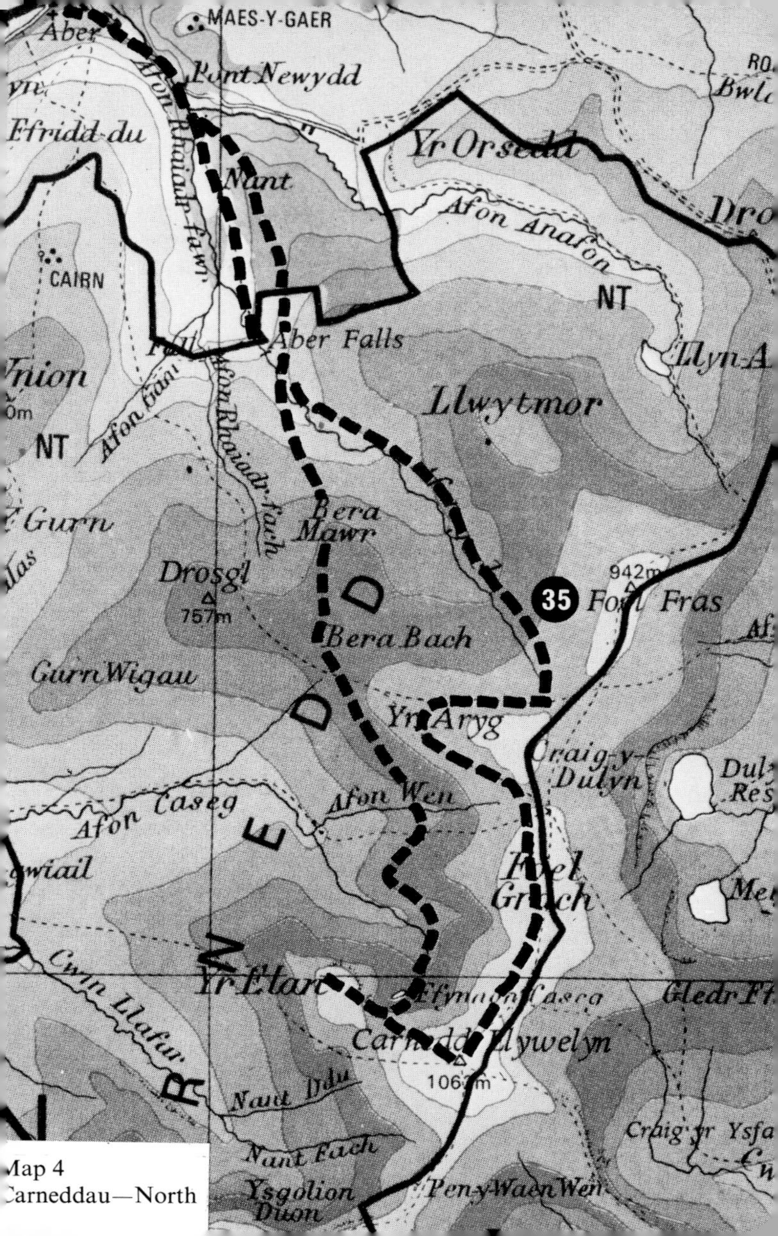

Map 4
Carneddau—North

Bera Mawr →

The Moel Siabod Group

Moel Siabod	872 metres	2860 feet
Moelwyn Mawr	770 metres	2526 feet
Moelwyn Bach	710 metres	2329 feet
Allt Fawr	698 metres	2290 feet
Cnicht	689 metres	2260 feet
Moel Druman	676 metres	2217 feet
Ysgafell Wen	672 metres	2204 feet
Moel yr Hydd	648 metres	2125 feet

OS Map: Landranger 115 Snowdonia
Outdoor Leisure 16/17 Snowdonia & Conwy Valley

The shapely peak of Moel Siabod is the northern sentinel of a vast upland area, dappled with lakes and tarns, that sprawls in a south-westerly direction to end with the Moelwyns in the east and Cnicht in the west. It is perhaps strange that the topography of the group reveals so few mountains worthy of attention, and were it not for the graceful tapering lines of the latter which, when seen end-on from the south-west is reminiscent of the Matterhorn, it might well escape the notice of walkers. As it is, there are few who tread its isolated summit, and fewer still who scale and traverse the more distant Moelwyns. Nevertheless, there is no doubt that the group as a whole affords grand walking country, and especially that part of it centred round the attractive blue of Llyn Edno.

Since Moel Siabod overlooks Capel Curig, this is the obvious starting point for its shortest ascent, but it should be borne in mind that owing to the easy gradient of its grassy slopes it may be ascended from many directions; the only exception being the precipitous south eastern side above Llyn y Foel.

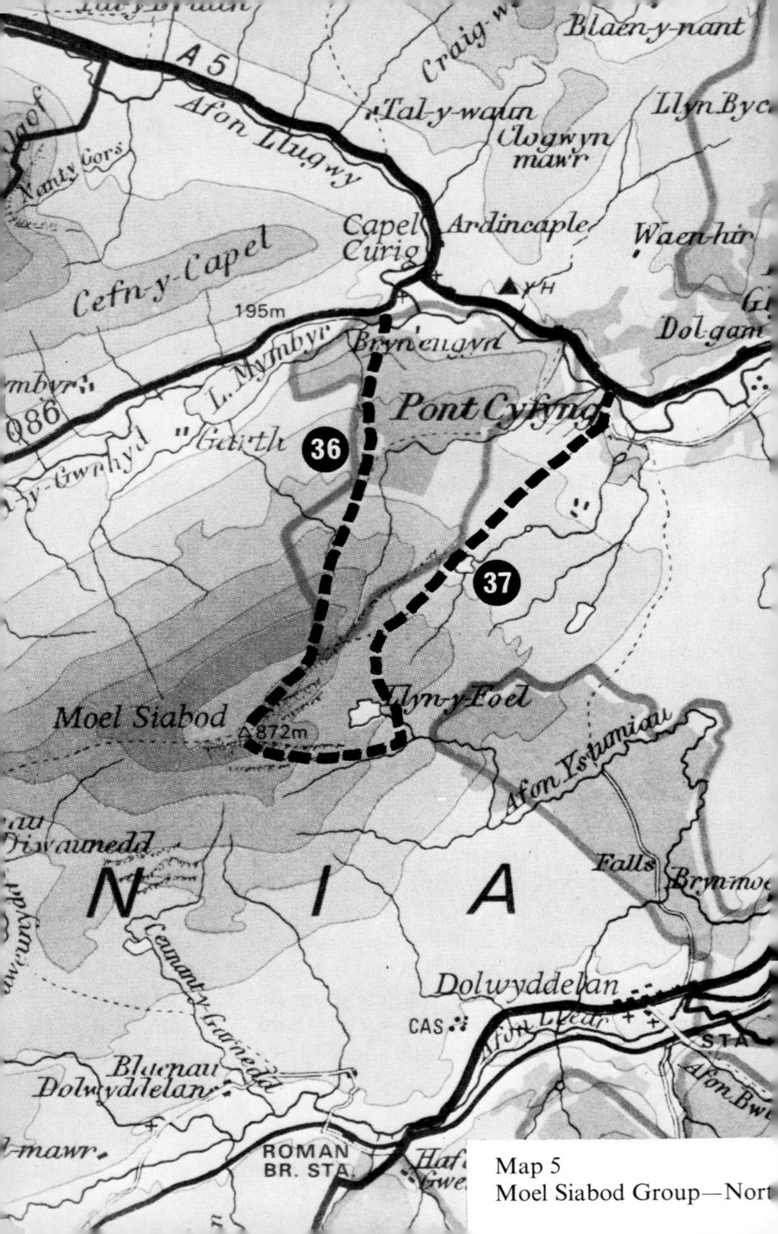

Map 5
Moel Siabod Group—Nort

Route 36. The Royal Bridge and Moel Siabod. Leave the village by the Royal Bridge, GR 716577, known locally as Pont y Bala, a wooden structure spanning the outflow of Llynnau Mymbyr, and note the splendid prospect of the Snowdon group R. Follow the path into the forest plantations clothing the lower hillside and mount the path that winds its upward way through them, eventually to emerge from the leafy canopy with the foreshortened view of the peak on the skyline ahead GR 713565. Now make your way almost straight to the ridge where a succession of large flat rocks deck the crest. There are sensational views L down the cliffs to Llyn y Foel. These rocks pave the way to the summit cairn standing amid a chaotic collection of boulders. A variation of this route goes L above the trees and eventually reaches the crest of the north-eastern ridge of the mountain which is climbed in its entirety. It has the advantage of spacious views on either hand during the greater part of the ascent.

The panorama from Moel Siabod is of exceptional interest owing to its isolated position on the eastern fringe of Snowdonia, and while its extensive views round the south-western arc will disclose both near and distant objects, including Dolwyddelan Castle below, it is the western prospect of a galaxy of peaks and valleys that will rivet the gaze. The Snowdon Group first catches the eye and on the L of Lliwedd appears the sharp cone of Yr Aran, with further L Moel Hebog and its satellites. Below them there are glimpses of Llyn Dinas and Llyn Gwynant. To the R of Snowdon rise the Glyders, with both Bristly Ridge and the top of Tryfan prominent above the intervening ridge, and with further R the conspicuous sloping top of Pen yr Ole Wen leading the eye to the tremendous landscape of the Carneddau, where Carnedd Llywelyn appears above the falling craggy ridge of Gallt yr Ogof.

Moel Siabod ←

Plate 155 Variations of **Route 36**

Carnedd Ugain

Snowdon

Cwm Dyli

Lliwedd

Yr Aran

Llyn Gwynant

Moel Hebog

Llyn Dinas

Route 37. Cyfyng Falls, Llyn y Foel and Moel Siabod. This is the finest and most rewarding ascent of the dominating peak of the group, because it unfolds a close view of its precipitous south eastern front, an aspect that is not clearly revealed from more distant viewpoints.

Walk down the road from Capel Curig and turn R over the stone bridge spanning Cyfyng Falls. GR 734573. These are worthy of notice when the Afon Llugwy is in spate and a good viewpoint will be found farther down the highway. Avoid the first fork R over the bridge, but bear R at the second and ascend the old quarry road which, on emerging from the trees, passes an attractive farmhouse R. GR 733568. Thereafter continue along the now grassy road across the open moor, with views R of Capel Curig below and of the subsidiary top of Moel Siabod straight ahead. You must ensure that you stay strictly to the marked path all the way. Now go ahead past a small tarn L until the old slate quarry buildings are reached, from which you continue over a rise ahead and Llyn y Foel will come into view, hemmed in R by the rocky bastions of the peak. Walk L round the tarn and pass its outflow to gain the foot of the broken ridge GR 714545 rising to the summit of Moel Siabod. Climb along the edge of the crags for the view down into the wild cwm R and find a way in and out of the rocks and boulders until the cairn appears suddenly on the skyline.

Those who wish to, may by pass Llyn y Foel and strike out R for the north east ridge just a little before the small tarn GR 724558 below the main quarry.

Plate 157 **Route 37**—Cyfyng Falls in spate

Plate 158 **Route 37** and variation

Moel Siabod

Llyn y Foel

Plate 160 Cnicht from Tan-lan

Llyn Edno

Moel Meirch →

Passing place for cars; no parking

Crib Goch

Crib y Ddysgl

Snowdon

Llyn Edno

Plate 162 **Route 38**

Route 38. Cnicht by the Dog Lakes. This is one of the most delightful walks in the whole group and allows plenty of time for browsing in the heather beside one or other of the lovely tarns that are passed on the way. A car is useful for getting to Nantmor, because it not only saves time which may be spent more pleasantly on the higher ground, but it also facilitates the descent of Cnicht by reversing Route 40 if the vehicle is driven round to Croesor.

Drive along the charming Vale of Gwynant and turn south for the sequestered valley of Nantmor by crossing the bridge that spans the Afon Glaslyn near Bryn Dinas. GR 626503. Drive carefully up the steep and narrow road between stone walls. At its highest point the road turns sharp R near two gates. There is limited parking along this stretch of the road so you must go further along to park at some disused quarries. GR 633485. Walk back to the sharp bend and go through the gate R GR 637495 to reach the Afon Llyn Edno which is followed R uphill all the way to its source. The immediate ascent is the steepest and roughest section of the walk, and passes through a number of romantic little gorges on the slopes of Moel Meirch L. It is worthwhile to look back from time to time, since the scene discloses the twisting course of the lower section of the Watkin Path, dominated by Bwlch Main and Snowdon, with L a view of Llyn Dinas and of Moel Hebog and some of its satellites.

This route is the only sure way to locate Llyn Edno, because it is cradled in a shallow basin dappled with crags, and from other directions may be difficult to find; it is said to be full of trout and the local fishermen's paradise. Halt here awhile to enjoy the fine view and note the excellent prospect of the Snowdon Horseshoe to the north-west, where Yr Wyddfa appears above Lliwedd and the ridge R encompasses Crib y Ddysgl, the Pinnacles and Crib Goch. Before leaving this secluded and enchanting spot, walk round the south shore of the lake for the vista across it of Moel Siabod whose graceful lines are especially pleasing to the eye. Extensive marshes lie

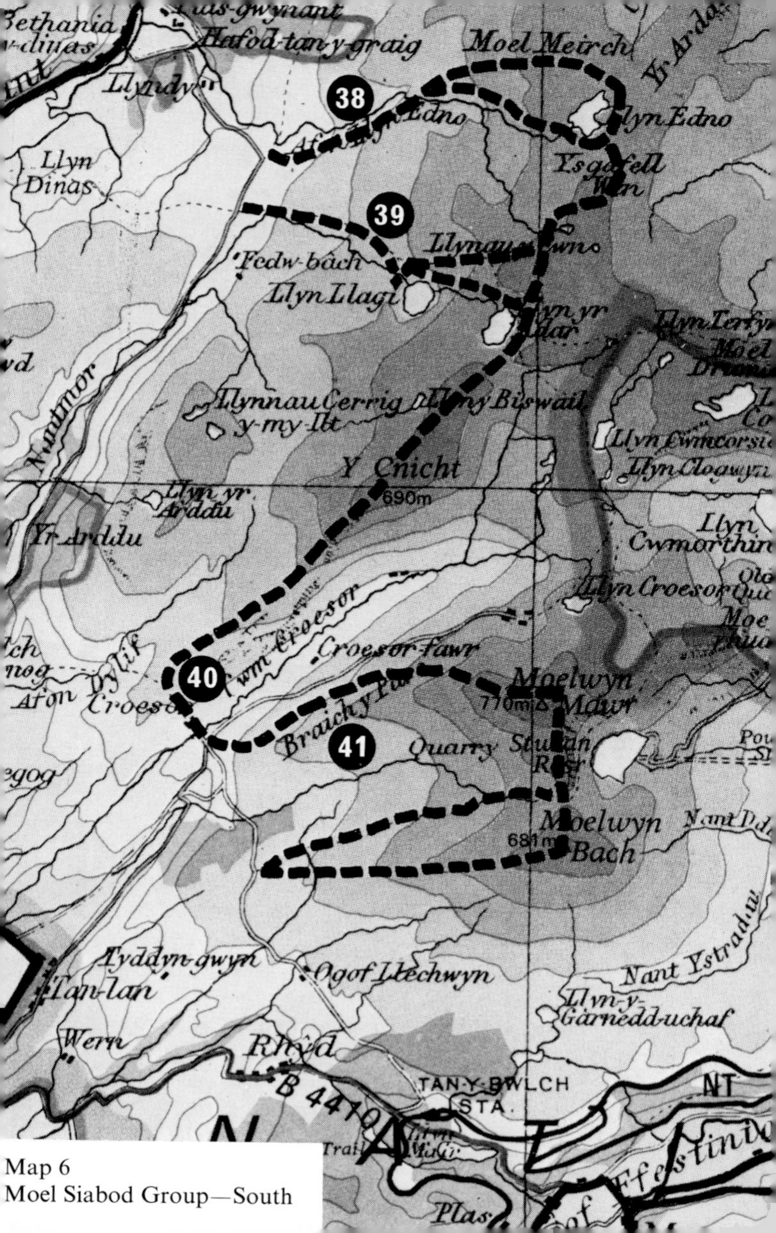

Map 6
Moel Siabod Group—South

Yr Aran

Cwm y Llan

Llyn Dinas

Plate 164 **Route 38**—Panorama from Cnicht

Moel Hebog   Craig Cwm Silyn   Nantlle Ridge   Y Garn II   Mynydd Mawr

Summit Ridge of Cnicht

Plate 166 **Route 38**—Panorama from Cnicht

to the east, and are the source of the Afon Lledr, which, after passing Dolwyddelan with its famous castle, flows into the River Conwy in the vicinity of Betws-y-coed.

Now ascend the nearby curving ridge of Ysgafell Wen which encloses these marshes, and walk south along its crest to the Dog Lakes, a collection of tiny tarns GR 663487. It also unfolds another excellent view of the Horseshoe, in which the precipitous eastern front of Yr Wyddfa is now clearly disclosed. Then go ahead past Llyn yr Adar R, and above Llyn y Biswail also R, to reach the base of the long summit ridge culminating in Cnicht. There are a few ups and downs on its crest and the cairn stands at its far end, overlooking Tremadoc Bay. By following this route to the peak its most surprising and striking feature is revealed in the sudden precipitous drop into Cwm Croesor, which gives the impression of perhaps 1000 metres whereas in fact it is only about 500 metres. Beyond rise the Moelwyns, whose graceful sweep is marred by unsightly and disused quarry workings. The panorama round the southern arc is extensive, with Tremadoc Bay seemingly almost at one's feet, the Harlech Dome L backed by the distant cliffs of Cadair Idris, and the Arans and Arenigs still farther L. But it is the vast panorama of Snowdonia that will hold the gaze, for this lofty and isolated peak is so placed that it reveals a chain of mountains that stretch right round the north-western arc. It is perhaps the finest coign of vantage in the whole region. The Moel Hebog group L comprises the reigning peak, the Nantlle Ridge and Mynydd Mawr; the centrally situated Snowdon group assumes graceful lines with views into Cwm Llan where the Watkin Path is clearly seen in a limpid atmosphere; the skyline R comprises the Glyders, Pen Llithrig y Wrach in the Carneddau, and ends with the nearer peak of Moel Siabod.

Note: It is possible to avoid the lower gorges of the Afon Llyn Edno by going through the gate and following the road on the R to the farm of Hafodydd Brithion. GR 640494. Beyond it follow a sketchy track that ultimately joins Route 38 near a sheepfold in more open country.

Route 39. Cnicht by Llyn Llagi. This is a shorter variation of Route 38 and its starting point is at the slate quarry, as for Route 38, where there is room for several vehicles. Walk back along the road to a converted chapel and take the track east towards an enchanting stone cottage. GR 637490. Pass to the L behind it to reach a gate beside the cascading stream. Continue ahead by a cairned path, with the murmuring stream R, and follow it all the way to its source in Llyn Llagi. Cross several walls *en route* and when the gradient eases off walk by the wall R across the grass to the lake. This remarkable circular sheet of water has a sombre and wild setting, and steep crags enclose its far side, broken in one place only by a perfectly straight gully that carries down the outflow from Llyn yr Adar, 200 metres above. There is an excellent camping site at its base, from where experienced scramblers may tackle the gully direct. The easiest way is to ascend the grassy hillside to the L of the wall and turn south along the skyline. GS 6548. On reaching Llyn yr Adar, pass round it and join Route 38 for Cnicht.

Plate 168 **Route 39**—Seen from the Chapel

Llyn yr Adar

Plate 170 **Route 39**—The Snowdon Group from Llyn yr Adar

Route 40. Cnicht from Croesor. This ascent is a pleasant walk and it begins at Croesor. This tiny secluded hamlet is encircled by green hills and reached by a narrow road from Garreg, a village on the eastern flanks of the Glaslyn Valley. Access to the side road is gained by a sharp turn at the attractive lodge of Plas Brondanw. GR 615420.

Leave your vehicle in the car park on R in the village GR 631447 and follow the road on the L of the chapel and then a cart track uphill until a level gap in the ridge is attained. Here the cart track bifurcates GR 628451 and you must take the R branch (there is also a sketchy track rising in a similar direction) and after passing a ruined building, cross a field and climb over a stile on the L of the gate. Then keep to the grassy track which bears R and soon attains a low break in the broad ridge. Here cross the stile on the L and go straight ahead to the foot of the mountain that now towers overhead. The route lies over private land and you should make every effort to follow the direction indicators. The ridge is reached quickly by taking this line, and on attaining it you are confronted by a rocky eminence surrounded by a high stone wall. It is advisable to pass through a gap on the R, descend slightly and then attain the ridge beyond it.

Keep to the ups and downs of the grassy track which takes a direct line for the peak. The last section is steep and there are two alternative routes: that L is the more popular because it includes some easy scrambling over rock and scree; that R is easier, grassy and less sensational, but joins the other just below the cairn. There is an annual race up and down this route, the record for which was set in 1994 by former British Fell running champion Colin Donnelly – it stands at a remarkable 32 minutes and 34 seconds. The ladies record, set in 1988, is held by Angela Carson at 37 minutes and 45 seconds.

Plate 171 **Route 40**—Cnicht comes into view here

Plate 172 **Route 40**—Easy walking to the final ascent

Plate 173 **Route 40**—The steepest section of the ridge rising to
Cnicht

Moelwyn Bach →

Craig Ysgafn →

Moelwyn Mawr →

Route 41. The Moelwyns from Croesor. These hills comprise three tops fairly close together and they make a fine skyline when seen from the Afon Glaslyn on the west side of the valley. Unhappily, the northern slopes of Moelwyn Mawr are spoilt by unsightly and now disused quarry workings, and of the many possible routes to the peak this ascent is chosen because it does not disclose them until the summit cairn is attained.

Leave transport in the car park at Croesor as for route 40 and return to the cross roads at the entrance to the hamlet. Go straight ahead, or if coming from Garreg turn sharp R, and beyond the first gate on the single-track road going over the low hills to Tan y Bwlch. GR 635440. Then turn L and ascend the grassy slopes beside a stone wall, and on reaching the top of this rise the Moelwyns come into view ahead. Now bear L and cross a wall by a convenient stile, and then go straight on over grass by a very indistinct track to the ridge L that rises to Moelwyn Mawr. It is clearly marked by a wire fence that runs up to a conspicuous stone tower, probably used long ago in connection with the quarry R of the peak. Finally ascend the steep shaly slopes above and follow the craggy rim of the cwm to attain the cairn at the far end of the ridge.

On a clear day the panorama round the north-western arc is of the first order and not unlike that already described from Cnicht, save that this mountain is in a direct line with Snowdon and therefore obscures the lower reaches of Cwm Llan. However, it has a unique feature in that immediately to the north the blue of some twelve tarns is disclosed in the sunlight and there is also a striking view of Moel yr Hydd R. Moreover, there is a spacious prospect of the sea byond Porthmadog and the southern arc reveals the Arenigs, the more distant Berwyns and the great mass of the Harlech Dome, backed by the cliffs of Cadair Idris. Now descend the grassy slopes to Craig Ysgafn, whose craggy summit is well seen from Moelwyn Mawr. Keep L over this very rough top and note the conversion

← Moel Hebog

Nantlle Ridge →

← Moelwyn Mawr

Plate 176 **Route 41**

Plate 177. Summit ridge of Moel yr Hydd, looking south-west over Moelwyn Mawr (left) to Cnicht. Beyond lie Moel Hebog, Nantlle Ridge and Mynydd Mawr.

of Llyn Stwlan into a reservoir far below, with Blaenau Ffestiniog beyond. Descend the steep terminal crags of this eminence
L, with steep drops also L, and follow the track down to the
col, Bwlch Stwlan, GR 660441. Then go ahead and climb
Moelwyn Bach by grass and crags L, or by easy grass slopes R,
and walk over to the last cairn which opens up a superb
prospect of all the peaks in Mid Wales. The easiest way off this
peak is to keep to the broad grassy ridge descending west all
the way to the road at GR 634433 and so back to Croesor. Do
not attempt to shorten the route by descending R into the vast
hollow, as it is dappled with bog and extensive stretches of
marshy ground, beyond which several walls and fences have
to be crossed to reach the road.

Plate 178. **Route 41** Over the Moelwyns

Moelwyn Bach

Craig Ysgafn

Moelwyn Mawr

The Moel Hebog Group

Moel Hebog	782 metres	2565 feet
Craig Cwm Silyn	734 metres	2408 feet
Trum y Ddysgl	709 metres	2326 feet
Garnedd Goch	700 metres	2296 feet
Mynydd Mawr	698 metres	2290 feet
Mynydd Drws-y-coed	695 metres	2280 feet
Moel yr Ogof	655 metres	2148 feet
Mynydd Tal y Mignedd	653 metres	2142 feet
Moel Lefn	638 metres	2094 feet
Y Garn II	633 metres	2076 feet

OS Map: Landranger 115 Snowdonia
         Outdoor Leisure 17 Snowdonia & Conwy Valley

Moel Hebog completely dominates the charming village of
Beddgelert, which occupies the floor of the valley at the three
cross-roads and effectively shelters it from the prevailing
south-westerly winds. Its elevation is foreshortened from this
near viewpoint, but its shapely stature is seen to greater
advantage from the bridge over the Afon Glaslyn half a mile
north of the village and better still from the more distant head
of Llyn Dinas when it is framed between the hills enclosing the
lower stretches of the Vale of Gwynant. Its finest elevation,
however, is revealed from Pont Cae'r-gors which spans the
Afon Colwyn some two miles north on the road to Caernarfon
when its graceful tapering lines are especially attractive by late
afternoon light. The ascent of this mountain makes a pleasant
and easy afternoon walk, but if its immediate satellites, Moel
yr Ogof and Moel Lefn, are included, then a full day is
necessary for most walkers.

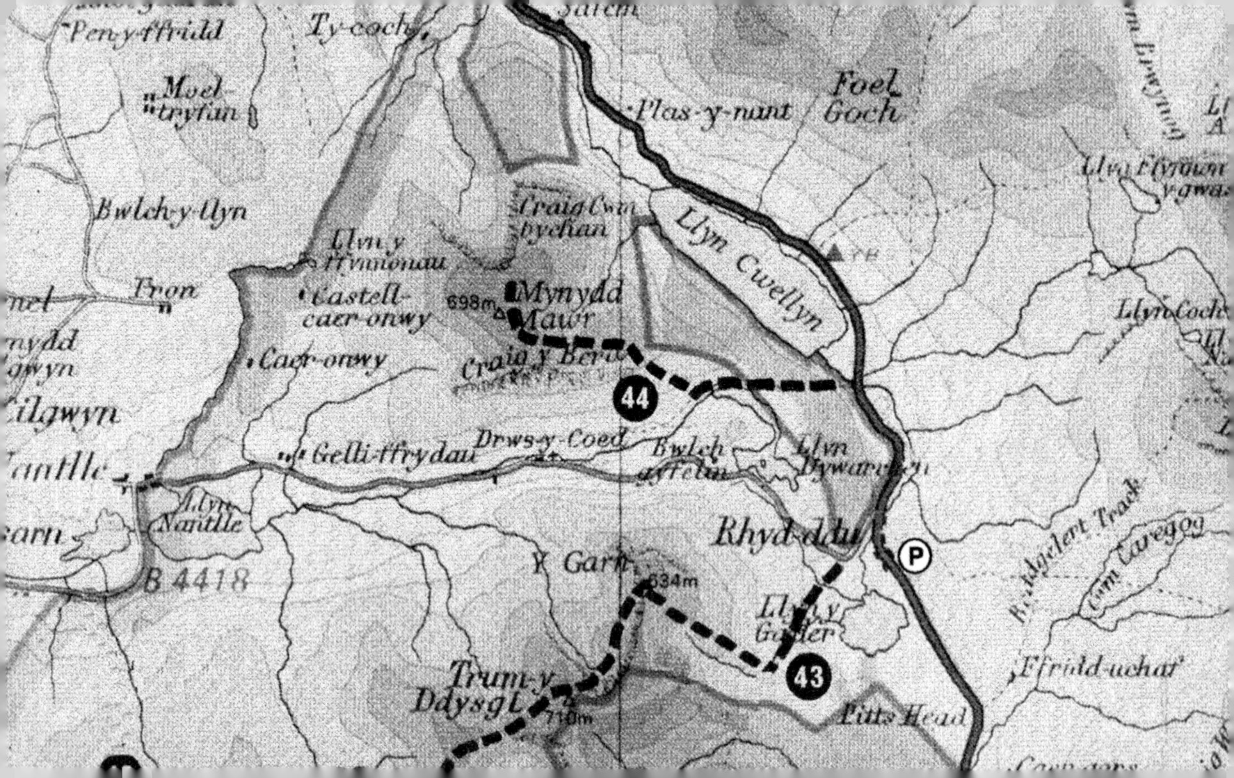

Pen-y-ffridd
Ty-coch
Moel-tryfan
Plas-y-nant
Foel Goch
Bwlch-y-llyn
Craig Cwm bychan
Llyn Cwellyn
Llyn y Ffynnonau
Tron
Castell-caer-onwy
698m
Mynydd Mawr
Llyn Coch
Caer-onwy
Craig y Bera
44
Cilgwyn
Drws-y-Coed
Gelli-ffrydau
Bwlch-gyfelin
Llyn Dywarchen
Llyn Nantlle
Rhyd-ddu
P
Y Garn
634m
B 4418
Llyn y Gader
Beddgelert Track
Cwm Caregog
Ffridd-uchaf
Trum-y Ddysgl
710m
43
Pitts Head

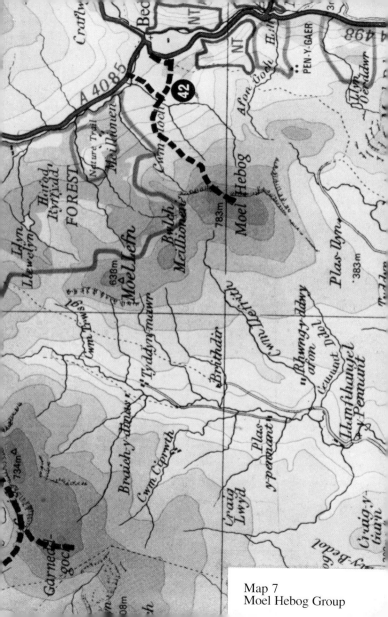

Map 7
Moel Hebog Group

Moel Hebog →

Plate 170. Stereo-pair print of **Route 43** from Cwm Clock

Route 42. Beddgelert and Moel Hebog. Cars can be parked in the main carpark in the centre of the village. The key to this route is the farmhouse of Cwm-cloch, GR 584482, which may be reached by a finger posted path through the fields behind the Royal Goat Hotel, or by going a short distance up the Caernarfon road and turning L over the Afon Colwyn. This bridge gives access to a by-road that passes under the long-disused Welsh Highland Railway and thence through a small pine wood to the farm. Go through a gate beside a farm building opposite and cross the usually wet pasture by a line of flat stones to a break in its far wall, beyond which a well marked path rises through heather and bracken. A large cairn, built on an immense boulder, will be observed high up the slope ahead and this is the key to the turning point in the route. It stands on a broad ridge in sight of the plantations and like many others on this mountain is flecked with white quartzite. It is worthwhile to pause here, if only to scan the scene round the northern arc, because, strange as it may seem, many of the engirdling hills look more imposing from this viewpoint than they do from the higher summit cairn. Although the Snowdon group should hold the gaze, it does not do so owing to its less interesting southern aspect. In consequence the eye wanders R to skim along the lovely stretches of the Vale of Gwynant in which the blue of Llyn Dinas contrasts beautifully and especially so in autumn, with its enclosing hills, to rest finally upon the lovely outline of Moel Siabod. Farther R Cnicht and the Moelwyns stretch across the skyline above the sylvan approach to the Aberglaslyn Pass, when the sharper elevation of Moelwyn Mawr from this angle will catch the eye. Now turn L at this key cairn and climb the ridge to a gate in a wall, where a line of cairns lead uphill to the L corner of the precipitous front of the peak. Then bear R and scramble up its rocky edge to the summit.

The cairn on Moel Hebog stands some distance back from its precipitous front and thus opens up the south-western prospect

Moel Hebog

Cwm-Cloch

of Cardigan Bay to advantage. The engirdling hills slope down gently to its shore and disclose among other eminences a fine outline of the Rivals away to the west. But to observe the northern arc it is advisable to descend slightly as Beddgelert is then disclosed over 600 metres below, backed by the Snowdon group and the Vale of Gwynant, a grand scene indeed.

Those wishing to extend this walk may do so by descending to the north along the ridge leading to Moel yr Ogof GR 557478 and continue for a further kilometre or so north-west to Moel Lefn. This top opens up a spacious prospect of the Pennant Valley L and of the Nantlle Ridge to its R. Continue the descent to the pass below and follow the path above the plantations to Rhyd Ddu, or bear R through them for a shorter return to Beddgelert. Walkers who know this route and might well prefer an alternative ascent, should leave their transport in the car park at the side of the A4085 near Nantmor GR 597462 and walk back to the bridge over the Aberglaslyn Gorge. Here turn L and walk about 100 metres to turn R on to a path through a gate and up the zigzags through the trees. Then pass through another gate on to the open hillside where bear R by the path for Oerddwr Uchaf, then keep R of the farm to a prominent cairn. Now proceed in a south-westerly direction to join Pant Paladr trackway and follow it through a gate in the wall. Continue ahead until a wall junction is encountered, whence turn R and climb beside it to the summit of Bryn Banog. GR 575456. This eminence opens up a fine panorama which includes Cnicht, the Moelwyns, Cwm Pennant and Llyn Cwm y Stradlyn, together with the more distant Rivals and Cardigan Bay, all dominated in the north-east by Snowdon and Lliwedd. Now descend south-west to the col and climb the steep grass and scree to the summit of Moel Hebog. Should you decide to descend to Beddgelert by Route 42, leave the village by the R bank of the Afon Glaslyn and cross the bridge of the old Highland Railway, from where you then walk through the tunnels back to your car.

Moel Hebog ←

Llyn Dinas

Plate 182 Beddgelert from **Route 42**

Cnicht

Moelwyns

Aberglaslyn Pass

Key Cairn

An exhilarating ridge walk, known as the Pennant Horse-shoe, combines the traverse of the two satellites of Moel Hebog with a section of Route 43. It starts in Cwm Pennant at Pont-y-Plas GR 530459, rises to Moel yr Ogof and follows the ridge to Moel Lefn. Thence there is a considerable loss in height before reaching a stile which gives easy access to the ascent of Trum y Ddysgl. On attaining the cairn Route 43 is followed to Garnedd Goch, whence the descent to Pont-y-Plas is made by Cwm Ciprwth.

Route 43. The Nantlle Ridge. The walk in either direction over the hills forming this interesting and revealing ridge, which encloses Drws-y-coed Pass on the south, is doubtless the finest in this group and compares favourably with some of the better known ones in Snowdonia. Its remote situation on the western fringe of the region makes it a prize for the connoisseur.

Since transport to either end of the ridge is desirable, and, moreover, as it is possible to walk there and back along its crest in a long day, it is a question of deciding at which end to begin and where to leave the vehicle, unless, of course, it can be arranged to have a car at either end. Those who are interested in photography will find the light favourable for an east-west traverse in the morning and also for the return in the afternoon, but others who wish to engage in rock climbing on the great slab in Cwm Silyn would do better to leave their transport at that end. Furthermore, not only is it easier to attain the ridge by first climbing Craig Cwm Silyn, but this course avoids the longer circuitous climb to the cairn on Y Garn II. If the latter ascent is chosen, then the car should be parked in Rhyd Ddu. But if the former, then it should be driven past Llyn Nantlle Uchaf, along the first fork L to the hamlet of Tan yr Allt, and then sharp L up a narrow twisting mountain road that ends in a field beyond a farm L GR 496511, where it may be parked within easy reach of Cwm Silyn.

Plate 184 Snowdon from the slabs of Y Garn II

Y Garn II

Mynydd Mawr

Craig-y-Bera

Llyn y Gadair

Plate 185 **Route 43**–First section

Mynydd Drws-y-coed

Y Garn II

To Bwlch
Gylfin

PATH
To Cwm Pennant ONLY
FOLLOW ARROWS

On the assumption that one carries a camera, I shall describe the Nantlle Ridge from east to west, but it should be understood that some of my studies illustrating this route were in fact taken on the return walk. Access to these peaks is a delicate affair and you should pay heed to the advice that follows. Park in Rhyd Ddu at the main Snowdon car park GR 571524.

The mountain can only be climbed by first walking along the path towards Pennant. This leaves the road at a gate on the L about one kilometre from Rhyd Ddu, GR 566526, at the first sharp bend to Bwlch Gylfin. Follow the wall to a farm gate, from where you bear L uphill and follow the arrows in the direction of the distant plantations. Do not leave this path until you have crossed a stile, beyond which a largish boulder directs you to the L for Pennant and to the R for the ridge rising to Y Garn II. Now ascend this ridge by a sketchy track, cross another stile some way up the hill, whence climb over steep grass to the stony summit and cairn.

The extensive panorama from this lofty sentinel is justly magnificent and reveals the whole of the western aspect of the Snowdon group to perfection, with the village of Rhyd Ddu far below and R the cone of Yr Aran above the shimmering blue of Llyn y Gadair. To the north there is a fine view of the shattered crags of Craig y Bera on the other side of the pass, and below the rounded summit of Mynydd Mawr. To the west the first two tops surmounting the ridge are well seen and there are glimpses of the others R, with farther R Llyn Nantlle Uchaf and the sea, while to the south the broad ridge culminates in Moel Hebog.

Now turn your steps southwards and pick up the grassy track beside a stone wall L, pass the exit of a deep gully R, and start the rocky climb to the summit of Mynydd Drws-y-coed. GR 548517. Be careful near the top when turning L to step across a gap where rock projects above, and then keep to the edge of the summit cliffs with a big drop R. On the other side descend through crags and beyond the col follow the grassy

Rhyd Ddu

Plate 188 **Route 43**—Craig y Bera from Y Garn II

Mynydd Drws-y-coed

Plate 189 The trickiest section of **Route 43**

Craig Cwm Silyn   Mynydd Tal y mignedd

Plate 190 Ridges of **Route 43**, seen from Y Garn II

Craig Cwm Silyn

The Rivals

Mynydd Tal y mignedd

path to the summit of Trum y Ddysgl which opens up a good backward view of the ridge and of the immense cairn on Mynydd Tal y Mignedd. Continue down a long grass slope and make for the connecting ridge below, which has eroded so badly that the path descends L to pass this hiatus at the saddle. Then walk up to a short length of wall and go L of it to reach the conspicuous obelisk on this summit. It is so large that it can be seen from a great distance on a clear day and is said to have been built by quarrymen whose hobby was the erection of this pillar. The summit of Mynydd Tal y Mignedd GR 535514 opens up a fine prospect of Craig Cwm Silyn, with the narrow rock ridge rising to its cairn from Bwlch Dros Bern, a little used pass from Nantlle to Pennant. The distant Rivals can be seen R above the cwm, with a glimpse of one of the tarns below, and this viewpoint is one of the few from which the castles of Caernarfon, Criccieth and Harlech can be seen simultaneously. Continue the traverse by walking downhill towards the next peak on the ridge, and beyond the pass exercise care while climbing the rock ridge ahead, with steep drops L, until the cairn on Craig Cwm Silyn is attained. Rest here awhile to admire the superb retrospect which unfolds the whole of the undulating ridge, backed by Snowdon. Then continue westwards and bear R over a wilderness of rocks until Cwm Silyn appears below R and note the tremendous slab which is the venue of expert rock climbers, and beneath which are cradled the two glittering tarns. Descend the rim of the cwm and make for the locked gate, beyond which a grassy cart road leads direct to the car park. This is the usual terminus of the traverse, but those who wish to continue to Garnedd Goch from Craig Cwm Silyn may walk over a mile of almost level stony ground, past two large cairns, whence grass and a wall lead to the final cairn on the ridge.

Trum y Ddysgl

The Rivals

Cwm Silyn

Plate 193 Last ascent on **Route 43**

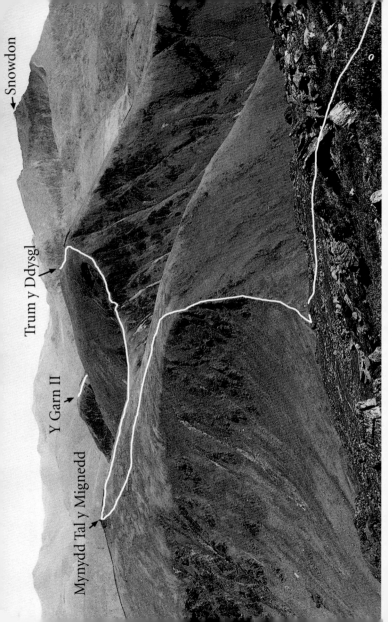

Snowdon

Trum y Ddysgl

Y Garn II

Mynydd Tal y Mignedd

Plate 195 **Route 43**—Optional extension and final descent

Plate 197 Cwm Silyn from **Route 43**

Route 44. Craig y Bera and Mynydd Mawr. Both Y Garn II and Craig y Bera are clearly visible from the road near Llyn y Gadair and the shattered crags of the latter overhang the northern slopes of Drws-y-coed Pass. To attain them and then continue to the summit of Mynydd Mawr is an afternoon excursion which can be started conveniently from Planwydd Farm, situated on the L of the road near the head of Llyn Cwellyn. GR 567539 A Forestry road threads the plantation, and opposite a building on the R a grassy break in the trees carries the power lines over the crest of the hill. This can be reached by a short cut uphill from the farm to a gate, from where the path runs almost level with the power lines. Follow this grassy path, and on reaching open ground overlooking the Nantlle Valley turn R by the wire fence and continue along the path, crossing the stiles provided. Then ascend the steep grass of Foel Rudd GR 548544 which forms the prominent shoulder of the peak, and from which the retrospect of Snowdon and Llyn Cwellyn below is worth noting. Thereafter keep to the path which passes to the R of Craig y Bera as shown in Plate 200. Here you may rest awhile to observe the scene of chaos at your feet and of the ups and downs of the Nantlle Ridge on the other side of the pass, now far below. Then follow the track which rises at an easy gradient over stony ground until the cairn on Mynydd Mawr appears on the skyline. The extensive flat summit discloses Anglesey and the sea to the north, but limits the appraisal of the vast panorama of hill and valley in other directions. Snowdon is, of course, supreme, and L appear Glyder Fawr with a glimpse of Tryfan over its shoulder, then Y Garn encloses the higher tops of the Carneddau between them, while R of Snowdon the skyline encompasses both Cnicht and the Moelwyns.

An alternative descent may be made by way of Craig Cwm Bychan. On attaining its summit cairn, walk down heathery slopes in a south-easterly direction to a stream which follows below the climbing face of Castell Cidwm. Here you bear R, but before reaching the shore of Llyn Cwellyn pick up the forestry track on the R and walk along it all the way back to Planwydd Farm.

Note: At the time of writing there is no parking space near Planwydd Farm, but a car can be left either at Rhyd Ddu or near the Snowdon Ranger Youth Hostel, both of which involve a long walk to the starting point of this route.

Craig y Bera

Crag y Bera

Mynydd Mawr

Llyn y Dywarchen

Plate 199 Upper section of **Route 44**

Mynydd Mawr

Craig y Bera

Llyn y Dywarchen

Plate 201 **Route 44**—The precipices of Craig y Bera

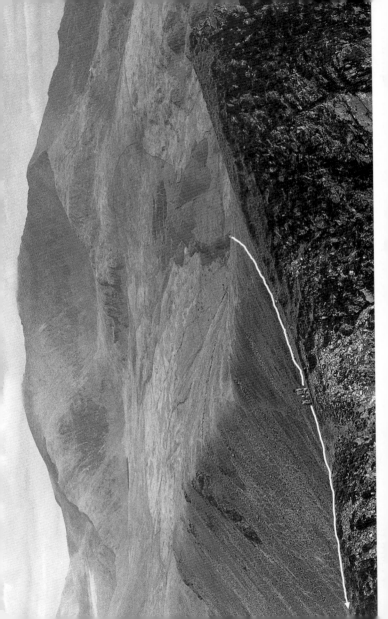

Y Garn II

Plate 203   The Nantlle ridge from **Route 44**

Cadair Idris

Pen y Gadair	893 metres	2929 feet
Mynydd Moel	863 metres	2831 feet
Craig y Cau	762 metres	2500 feet
Gau Graig	683 metres	2240 feet
Tyrau Mawr	661 metres	2168 feet
Craig Las	661 metres	2168 feet
Craig Llyn	622 metres	2040 feet
Bwlch Rhiwgwrefydd	560 metres	1838 feet
Llyn y Gadair	560 metres	1837 feet
Llyn y Cau	473 metres	1552 feet
Llyn y Gafr	427 metres	1400 feet

OS Map: Landranger 124 Dolgellau & surrounding area
 Outdoor Leisure 23 Cadair Idris

Cadair Idris is one of the three chief mountains of Wales and ranks second only to Snowdon in popularity. Consisting of alternate strata of Felspathic trap and shale, it takes the form of a high ridge and extends for some eight miles between Cross Foxes on the east and Arthog on the west. Its northern front is precipitous and girt with crags which are broken in one or two places only; that of the scree slope carrying the Foxes' Path is the most noteworthy. Beneath the crags are ranges of foothills, and below these again lie the Mawddach Estuary and the town of Dolgellau. Several rugged spurs extend southwards from the ridge and give easy access to Tal y Llyn and the Dysynni Valley, but one of them bends eastwards to form a grand rocky cwm in the bosom of which rests the stygian waters of Llyn y Çau. This magnificent scene is frowned upon by the steep, riven crags of Craig y Cau, the whole forming one of the wildest places in all Wales: it is now a National Nature Reserve.

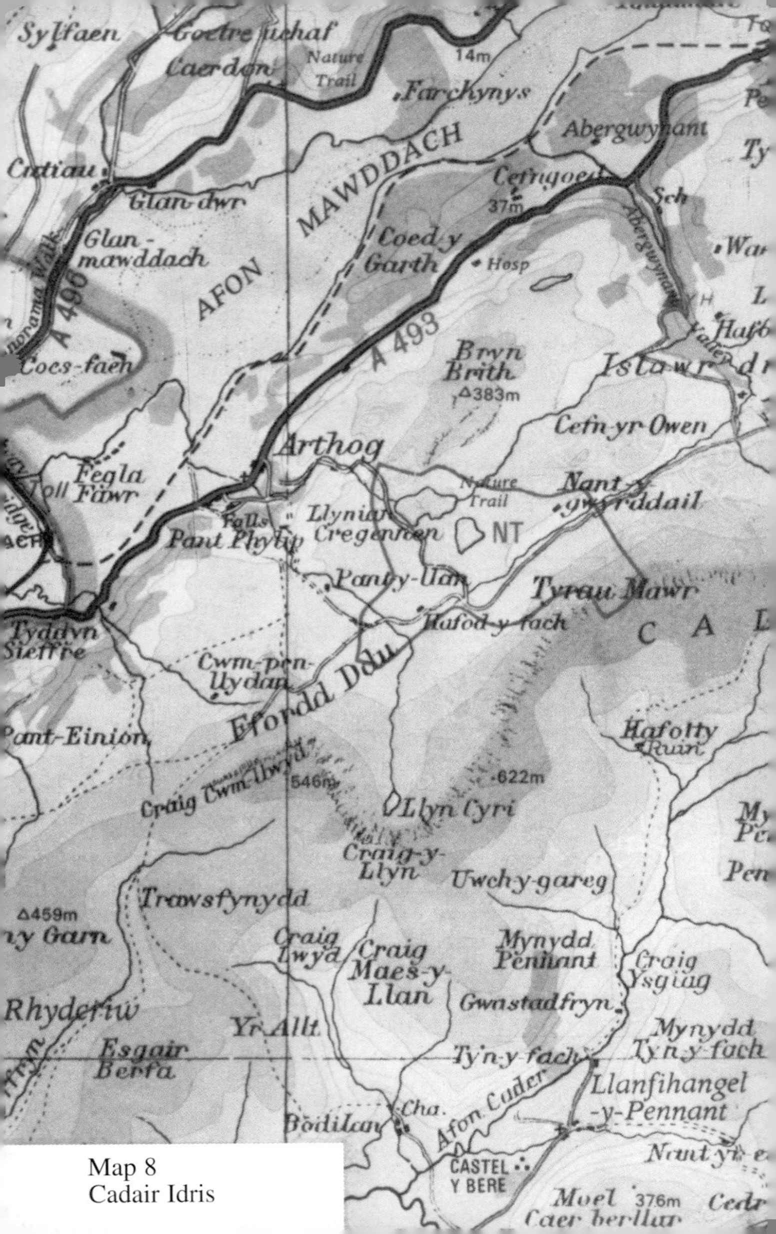

Map 8
Cadair Idris

Dolgellau
(Dolgelley)
Pandy
Afon Wnion
Bryn y gwin
Hendre gefeilliaid
Tyny clawdd
Gilfachwydd
Tir Stent
Afon Aran
Maes coch
Garth
Llyn y Gafr
Llyn Aran
Mynydd Moel
855m
Llyn y Gadair
893m
IDRIS
Mynydd 286m
Gwern graig
Craig y Llam
A 487
45
P
Mynydd Fron fraith
Minffordd
Fron frach
Hen gae
Ceiswyn
544m
Pentre
Craig Ddu
Dol-ffanog
Craig
Mynydd
Tal y llyn Lake
Tal y llyn
Mynydd Rugog
Aberllefeni
484m
Garnedd wen
574m
Corris Uchaf
Craig Goch

Cadair Idris is the traditional "Chair" of Idris, a giant whom the old bardic writings represent as having been at once poet, astronomer and philosopher, and who, moreover, is alleged to have studied the stars from his rocky seat on the summit of this peak. The chair is the gigantic hollow immediately to the north of Pen y Gadair and is hemmed in on the east by the Foxes' Path, and on the west by the narrow, shattered ridge of Cyfrwy. It cradles the lonely waters of Llyn y Gadair.

The extraordinary popularity of the mountain is due in part to its accessibility and ease of ascent from all points, but more especially to the extensive panorama unfolded to the north from the entire length of its crest. This superiority of outlook is accounted for by its position in relation to the Mawddach Estuary and the valleys extending towards to Trawsfynydd Lake in the north and Bala Lake in the north-east.

Route 45. Tal y Llyn, Cwm y Cau and Pen y Gadair. There are at least eight routes of ascent, three from each side of the ridge and one from each end of it, but the finest of them all is that from Tal y Llyn. There is a car park at the junction of the A487 and the B4405 near Minffordd GR 733115. The beginning of the path is clearly signposted from here and the early part of the walk is along an avenue of conifers, which in spring is embellished by colourful rhododendron blossoms. Cross a bridge and then a stile, and turn R to ascend the path that rises steeply through trees beside the stream coming down from Llyn y Cau. Much work has been undertaken to combat the effects of erosion here so do please stay on the path. Pass the precipitous, rocky bluff of Ystradgwyn that is shagged with conifers R, and on emerging from the leafy canopy the path rises through bracken L. Remain on the true R bank of the stream and soon you will be surprised by a sudden view of the broken cliffs of the immense crag of Craig y Cau together with the detached obelisk of the Pencoed Pillar, rising above a boulder-strewn ridge that encloses the tarn hidden at its feet.

Now advance over stony ground and make for the R corner of the tarn, where a conspicuous boulder is poised beside its outflow. This point unfolds a splendid near-view of Craig y Cau, whose shattered front of buttresses, gullies and grassy terraces all rise diagonally R to peter out below the skyline. On the extreme R there is a Stone Shoot that affords a quick descent to the tarn, but is not recommended in ascent. The crags of this fine pyramid are a playground of the rock climber and a fine but difficult climb tackles the face of the Pencoed Pillar L, which is separated from the main cliff by the fearsome Great Gully.

Continue the ascent by heading south from the lake and then bear R to join the well-worn route. Climb this track which later gains the crest of the precipices enclosing the cwm to the north, and keep to its crest while enjoying the extensive views towards Tal y llyn L, whose shimmering blue is occasionally glimpsed through gaps in the folds of the hills. Note also the terrific cliffs of Pen y Gadair across the tarn R, and Cwm Amarch engirdled by crags L, with beyond it the long sloping ridge of Mynydd Pencoed, then walk up to the cairn on Craig y Cau.

After a well-earned rest on this breezy top, continue the walk by descending to the Col that joins this subsidiary peak to the main ridge of Cadair, and note in passing the head of the Stone Shoot R already mentioned. Pen y Gadair now towers into the sky ahead and its sharp, rocky summit crowns the long ridge stretching to east and west. The track skirts the crags of this peak, but on attaining the ridge leave it and bear L along the rim of the cwm that cradles Llyn y Gadair R until the cairn at the end of Cyfrwy is reached. The approach to the cairn is the best viewpoint for the appraisal of the tremendous terraced cliffs of Cadair and also for the long scree of the Foxes' Path L. It is, moreover, a safe place from which to observe the narrow broken ridge of Cyfrwy that falls to the conspicuous Table, part of the classic Cyfryw Arête climb. Now return along the edge

of the cliffs and climb to the summit of Pen y Gadair where there is a shelter just below the cairn and walkers can find a comfortable resting place on a cold and windy day.

When the atmosphere is clear the vast panorama of mountains, valleys, lakes and sea unfolded from this lofty perch is one of the finest in all Wales. The splendour of the northern arc discloses wide vistas of Cardigan Bay on the west with glimpses of Barmouth at the mouth of the Mawddach Estuary. The whole of Snowdonia may be seen far to the north beyond the intervening heights of the Harlech Dome, where Diffwys and the Rhinogs lead the eye to Yr Wyddfa R. The rounded summit of Rhobell Fawr is almost in line with the lonely Arennigs farther away on the open moorland, while to the north-east Bala Lake and the Arans are prominent on the extreme R. The southern arc is less spectacular and the eye is drawn to Plynlimon which may be perceived crowning the swelling moorland horizon.

For those who have arranged for a car to meet them at Llyn Gwernan you will descend the mountain by the Foxes' Path, which leaves the ridge some little distance to the north-east of the summit. On this descent you will pass both Llyn y Gadair and Llyn y Gafr on the way down and obtain remarkable retrospects of the long line of precipices in the late afternoon light. Those making for the Youth Hostel at Kings will take a westerly course along the ridge and descend at the saddle of Rhiw-gwredydd, or if preferred continue to Tyrau Mawr and skirt Craig Las to reach the road. Those who wish to return to Tal y llyn, however, have four routes open to them: they can return the way they came, but may shorten the walk by descending the Stone Shoot at the Col; from the top of Craig Cwm Amarch they can diverge R and traverse the crest of Cwm Amarch, to the south-west walking thence down steep grass slopes to the south, past a little shimmering tarn directly to Tal y Llyn lake; or, from the summit they can stroll eastwards along the first section of the ridge, but bear R before

← Cadair Idris

Bwlch Llyn Bach →

reaching Mynydd Moel and then go down a rather indistinct track beside a dilapidated stone wall to join the route of ascent above the trees; and the final choice is to continue along the entire length of the summit ridge to the end of Gau Graig, GR 743140 traversing Mynydd Moel en route, and thereafter descend carefully through the crags to the road near the top of the pass R. The latter is undoubtedly the finest course, with the Arans prominent on the north-eastern skyline all the way.

Stone Shoot →

← Craig y Cau

Pencoed Pillar →

Llyn y Cau

Plate 208 **Route 45**—Upper section seen from Craig y Cau

Cyfrwy →   Ridge ↘   Harlech Dome →   Snowdon ↘

←Table

Plate 210 **Route 45**—The Mawddach Estuary from Cyfrwy

The Harlech Dome

Y Llethr	756 metres	2480 feet
Diffwys	750 metres	2460 feet
Rhinog Fawr	720 metres	2362 feet
Rhinog Fach	712 metres	2335 feet
Moel Penolau	614 metres	2014 feet
Craig Ddrwg	590 metres	1937 feet
Llawllech	588 metres	1930 feet
Moel y Blithcwm	547 metres	1804 feet
Carreg y Saeth	440 metres	1442 feet
Bwlch Tyddiad	394 metres	1294 feet
Bwlch Drws Ardudwy	381 metres	1250 feet

OS Map: Landranger 124 Dolgellau & surrounding area.
Outdoor Leisure 18 Snowdonia – Harlech & Bala.

This is the long backbone of hills almost parallel with the coast of Mid-Wales which extends from north to south for a distance of some eighteen kilometres. Moel Penolau stands like a sentinel overlooking Tremadoc Bay in the north, while Llawllech forms the southern outpost of the ridge above Barmouth Bay. Y Llethr dominates the whole chain but is only marginally higher than its close neighbour, Diffwys. However, the two peaks which appeal more strongly to the walker are Rhinog Fawr and Rhinog Fach, because in clear weather the former reveals the whole of Snowdonia to the north, and both of them cradle a number of wildly situated tarns. Rhinog Fawr is bounded on the north by the famous Roman Steps and by the wild pass of Bwlch Tyddiad while the two peaks are separated by the desolate pass of Bwlch Drws Ardudwy. Moreover, they are some of the most rugged hills in the country and are strewn with large boulders and scree which, to make matters worse for the walker, are literally covered with waist-high heather.

Y Lleth

Llyn Hywel

754m

Llyn y M...

Rhinog Fach

711m

Llyn Cwm hosan

47

Llyn Morwynion

Afon Crawcwellt

Bwlch...

Craig...

Graig-isaf

Graig ddu uchaf

Llyn Du

677.0m

Roman Steps

Gloywlyn

Ogwy?n... wlch

Craig-y-Saeth

440...

Rhinog Fawr

Foel Ddu

Coed trafnant

Cwm Nantcol

Maes-y-garnedd

Gaer-fynog

Nantcol

Dol-bebin

Pont-y-bont

Pen-isa'r Pont cwm-nantcol

Tyddyn-buch

Gelli-bant

Cwm mawr

Cwm...

Cwm-y-...

46

Dol-wreiddiog

Gerddi-bluog

Cwm-y-nantcol

Afon Artro

Meuthyr

Moel-y-gerddi

380m

Moel y Sensigl 311m

STANDING STONE

Uwchyllan

Ffridd-llwyn-grual

Tyddyn-y-felin

Maes-yr-haelfawr

Hafod-y-llyn

Penarth

Gwern-Einion

Hafod y-cyd

Mature Trails

Llas Ynys

NT

MURIAU'R GWYDDELOD

Pen-sarn

Bryn-hyfryd

Croesflas

Llanfair

Pen-rhiw

Sarn Hir

Llanbedr

A49

Rhinog Fawr is easily ascended from the farm at the end of the narrow road beyond Llyn Cwmbychan, GR 645314 which may be reached from the village of Llanbedr situated on the main thoroughfare between Harlech and Barmouth. Rhinog Fach is most accessible from the farm of Maes-y-Garnedd GR 642270 which stands at the head of Nant Col and is the centre of the vast amphitheatre formed by the two mountains. It may also be reached from the same village by 6.5 kilometres of a narrow, twisting and many gated road. The following two tough routes disclose the finest scenery in the district, and include Llyn Perfeddau, Llyn Hywel and Llyn y Bi and Llyn Du, Gloywlyn and Llyn Cwmbychan, as well as the Roman Steps.

Special note *Parking is available on the east end of Llyn Bychan, GS6431 but while the narrow roads to Cwmbychan and Cwm Nantcol are negotiable by cars they should not really be used during the holidays nor throughout the summer because they clutter up the roads and passing bays as parking areas, making the movement of essential transport by the local farmers virtually impossible. Be a sport and leave your car in Llanbedr!*

Rhinog Fawr
Route 46. The Roman Steps and Rhinog Fawr. The delightful sylvan Vale of Artro extends from Llanbedr to Llyn Cwmbychan a quiet little tarn overhung by the rocks of Craig y Saeth R, where the rough hill road continues to the farm. Turn R over a bridge and follow the path through a coppice to emerge eventually on the craggy hillside. At this point it is necessary to keep a sharp look-out for the Roman Steps, which lead ultimately to Bwlch Tyddiad, GR 654303. It is easy to miss their longest and best stretch as the path runs below them for some distance. It begins on the other side of a stone wall and lies immediately beneath the crags enclosing the south side of the narrow defile. According to tradition the steps were constructed by the Romans to facilitate the ascent and descent of their sentries, but they are now ascribed to medieval times.

Bwlch Tyddiad

Plate 212 **Route 46**—The Roman Steps

Now walk along this ancient promenade to the crest of the pass and observe the featureless nature of the extensive moor of Trawsfynydd. Hereabouts the rugged spurs of Rhinog Fawr overhang too precipitously for their safe ascent, and it is better to go back until a weakness in the form of a steep watercourse appears in these ramparts. This is the easiest point at which to begin the toilsome ascent. Climb slowly and carefully between the large boulders almost hidden by heather for perhaps 100 metres height gain and then edge round a big buttress to reach Llyn Du. This desolate sheet of water occupies a striking situation on the northern flanks of Rhinog Fawr and is enclosed on the south by broken precipices which extend upwards to the top of the mountain. Scale the ridge at the west corner of the tarn eventually to attain the two cairns on the summit of this peak.

When the atmosphere is clear this relatively close and lofty coign of vantage opens up a remarkable prospect of Snowdonia to the north. The Moelwyns are the nearest, with glimpses of Cnicht L and Moel Siabod R, while Moel Hebog is prominent to the north-west, with much of the Nantlle Ridge L. Between these two groups of hills Snowdon and its satellites stand supreme, and R of them and above Gallt y Wenallt there is a distant glimpse of Y Garn and Glyder Fawr. The Rivals are conspicuous to the west beyond the blue of Tremadoc Bay, and the Arennigs appear across the moorland to the north-east. Due east this aspect of the Arans is disappointing, whereas to the south and above Y Llethr the long line of cliffs supporting Cadair Idris rivet the gaze.

The quickest descent would appear to be in a direct line with the glittering blue of Gloywlyn far below, but since the intervening slopes are littered with large boulders hidden by deep heather, the walk down involves many detours and may be rather tiring. The lake is cradled in a shallow basin to the south-east of Craig y Saeth and, as it is a favourite with local anglers, there is a well-trodden path from its shore right down to the farm in the valley.

Rhinog Fawr

Bwlch Drws Ardudwy

Rhinog Fach

Y Llethr

Route 47. Nantcol and Rhinog Fach. Those who drive from Llanbedr to Nantcol will be surprised at the number of gates that have to be opened and shut before the farm of Maes y Garnedd, GR643269, is reached. The narrow and sinuous hill road threading this valley gives access to perhaps a dozen farms which may account for these several closures. Ensure that all gates are closed securely after you have passed through them. Leave the farm and take a direct line for Y Llethr in the south-east, but keep L of its spur to reach Llyn Perfeddau which lies to the north of this mountain. It is cradled in a grassy hollow and reveals a fine view of Rhinog Fach, whose precipitous front towers into the sky to the north-east. On leaving the tarn take a direct line for the mountain and climb a stony gully that peters out on the shore of Llyn Hywel. This tarn occupies the floor of a deep hollow between Y Llethr and Rhinog Fach, and as it is wide open to the prevailing south-westerly winds it can be a wild and boisterous place. The scene is on the grand scale and one of the most awe-inspiring in this group of hills. To the north the broken crags supporting the summit of Rhinog Fach rise literally from a sea of boulders and scree; to the south the steep ridge of Y Llethr runs up to the skyline and its sharp edge consists of gigantic slabs of rock lying end-on at an angle of forty-five degrees, while its base sinks down into the depths of the lake.

The Col between the two peaks is the key to their ascent and to attain it walk first to the south side of the tarn and then scale a gully that slants up a break in the slabs of rock. There are ample hand and footholds and on reaching the skyline a wall is encountered, from which you can see the rippling surface of Llyn y Bi some distance below. A track runs beside this wall and gives access to most of the summits crowning this long line of hills, so if bound for Y Llethr turn R, or if for Rhinog Fach turn L where the wall terminates at the summit cairn.

Y Llethr

Llyn Perfeddau

Llyn Hywel

Rhinog Fach

The panorama unfolded from this mountain top is not dissimilar from that of its neighbour, save that the latter which is some 10 metres higher, obscures a part of the view of Snowdonia. Begin the descent by walking along the declining summit ridge, on which the path peters out at the small cairn at its terminus, and look down the dizzy precipices overlooking Bwlch Drws Ardudwy far below. Do not attempt to descend them, but bear L and scramble carefully down the western flanks of the peak, making for the tiny pool of Llyn Cwmbosan, GR 660277, then continue through boulders and heather until the pass is reached and then turn L to follow the stream down to Nantcol.

← Rhinog Fach

Bwlch Drws Ardudwy →

Maes-y-garnedd →

← Rhinog Fawr

Plate 216 **Route 47**—Rhinog Fach from Llyn Hywel

Plate 217 **Route 47**—Slabs of Y Llethr

Y Llethr

Llyn Hywel

Rhinog Fach

Plate 218 Retrospect of **Route 47**

The Arenigs

Arenig Fawr	854 metres	2801 feet
Arenig Fach	689 metres	2260 feet
Craig y Bychan	677 metres	2221 feet
Moel Ymenyn	549 metres	1801 feet
Llyn Arenig Fach	426 metres	1400 feet
Llyn Arenig Fawr	404 metres	1326 feet

OS Map: Landranger 124 Dolgellau & surrounding area
Outdoor Leisure 18 Snowdonia – Harlech & Bala

The Arenigs are two conspicuous hills dominating the barren stretches of moorland in the northern corner of Mid-Wales. Arenig Fawr is the higher and more shapely eminence while Arenig Fach is a mere rounded hump on the heathery wilderness to the north of it. Both of these mountains may be ascended without difficulty from any direction, but the latter is of little interest. Arenig Fawr, on the other hand, is an altogether thoroughly enjoyable outing. It rises immediately to the south-east of the western end of Llyn Celyn. The ascent is quite short beginning as it does, on the 330 metre contour.

The most direct route goes up a wide grassy hollow dappled with scree, whence the undulating ridge leads straight to the broad backbone of the summit, which falls to the south-east where it is embellished with a number of strange little peaks. This affords a favourite descent for those who traverse the mountain on the way from Arenig Station to the village of Llanuwchllyn, a distance of seventeen kilometres.

The only interesting and revealing ascent of Arenig Fawr involves a considerable detour to the south-east and skirts the shores of Llyn Arenig Fawr GS 8438. This lonely lake lies immediately below a number of outcropping buttresses which

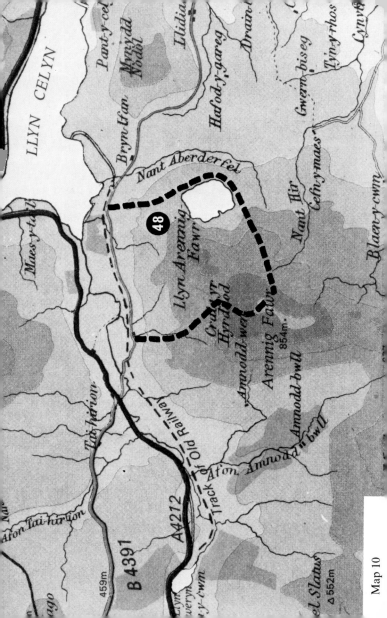

Map 10

are the occasional resort of the rock climber. From the southern end of the lake a rough ridge leads west to a grassy plateau that preludes the final slopes to the strange cairn on the summit of the mountain.

Arenig Fawr
Route 48. Bala, Llyn Arenig Fawr and Arenig Fawr. Leave Bala by the main highway to Ffestiniog, but when about one kilometre from the town turn L at the fork which is the old Arenig road. Pass a gate L that gives access to the open moor, where the white walls of a few tree-girt farmsteads afford some relief to the barren prospect. Continue ahead across the brown and green wilderness until the cottages clustered round the old Arenig Railway Station GR 841395 come into view. During the greater part of this journey Arenig Fawr dominates the scene, but the mountain disappears behind a craggy spur on the approach to the hamlet.

Park the car near the station and walk back along the road to a corrugated iron building R, then pass through a gate on to the open moor. Follow a track round the lower slopes of Gelli Deg R until the glimmering surface of Llyn Arenig Fawr appears ahead. Note the terraced outcrops of rock overhanging its west side, which are the occasional resort of the rock climber, but keep L round its shore. This remote tarn occupies one of the wildest and most desolate situations hereabouts and is in consequence seldom visited. Go ahead until its outflow is reached, where some piers and the dam constructed long ago confirm the conversion of the lake into a reservoir. Continue southwards and make for a rough ridge, Y Castell, GR 842373, that is supported by some bold terraced buttresses. Climb the steep slopes L and on attaining its crest Arenig Fawr is revealed on the western skyline. Now walk across the grassy plateau in a direct line with the cairn and ascend the last slopes to its summit.

The first object to attract the eye on this lofty peak will be the monument erected to commemorate the death of eight gallant Americans who crashed their Flying Fortress on August 4th, 1943, their machine having collided with the rocks a few feet below the western side of the summit. Then scan the vast panorama which on a clear day is very extensive owing to the isolated position of the mountain. Snowdon dominates the numerous prominent peaks on the north-western skyline; a glimpse of Bala Lake is disclosed to the south-east and is backed by the Berwyns; the twin tops of the Arans appear almost due south, with Rhobell Fawr on R, the latter being capped by the long cliffs of Cadair Idris; while the circle is completed in the south-west by the ridge of high hills crowned by Y Llethr.

Rest awhile to enjoy these revealing views and then begin the descent by walking due north-east along the broad backbone that extends from the summit. Bear L to reach the rocky terminus of Daear Fawr, spot height 697m GR 838383 which opens up a bird's-eye view of Llyn Arenig Fawr below to the east, and then head west to enter the wide grassy hollow that leads to the west of the old Arenig Station.

During this descent there are also spacious views of the reservoir in the vast Tryweryn Valley below, whose impounded water is allowed to follow the River Dee and is extracted into the water supply near Chester. It is called Llyn Celyn.

Arenig Fawr

Plate 220 **Route 48**—Llyn Arenig Fawr

The Arans

Aran Fawddwy	905 metres	2969 feet
Aran Benllyn	885 metres	2903 feet
Drws Bach	762 metres	2500 feet
Drysgol	730 metres	2397 feet
Camddwr	685 metres	2248 feet
Craig Cwm du	684 metres	2246 feet
Craig Cywarch	640 metres	2100 feet
Craig Ty-nant	614 metres	2014 feet
Creiglyn Dyfi	579 metres	1900 feet
Y Gribin	569 metres	1870 feet
Hengwm Rim	567 metres	1862 feet
Bwlch y Groes	545 metres	1790 feet
Llyn Lliwbran	472 metres	1550 feet
Craig y Geifr	457 metres	1500 feet
Moel Du	457 metres	1500 feet

OS Map: Landranger 125 Bala & Lake Vyrnwy

The rocky summit of Aran Fawddwy crowns the highest ridge south of Snowdonia: it attains an altitude of 905 metres, and is thus 12 metres higher than Cadair Idris, 19 metres higher than Pen y Fan, the dominating peak of the Brecon Beacons; and 153 metres higher than Plynlimon. The ridge is eight kilometres in length and Aran Fawddwy stands at its southern end, the northern outpost being Aran Benllyn, which overlooks Bala Lake.

These hills do not present an inviting aspect when viewed from the south and west and appear merely to crown a vast area of billowy moorland. If, however, Aran Benllyn is seen from Bala Lake its precipitous eastern front is disclosed, and this alone will tempt the mountaineer to climb it. On closer

Map 11
The Arans

inspection this line of black cliffs, flecked with white quartz and seamed with gullies, will be found to support almost the full length of the ridge. The only break is at its centre, where a grassy spur extends eastwards, its lower slopes cradling the circular tarn of Creiglyn Dyfi, which is the lonely birthplace of the River Dyfi.

Both of these peaks may be reached easily from a few points to the north, south and west of them, but their eastern flanks are not so accessible. The most interesting ascent, however, is that of Aran Fawddwy by way of the remote hamlet of Aber Cywarch, which lies a kilometre north east of Dinas Mawddwy. GS 8514. Here a narrow farm road diverges L of the highway and rises sharply between the cottages. It then threads a valley patterned with green fields and watered by the Afon Cywarch and, taking a north-westerly direction, ends at the farm of Cae Peris, which is situated immediately below the frowning cliffs of Craig Cywarch. A footbridge marks the commencement of the best route to Aran Fawddwy, and ascends over grass before joining the old peat track that rises diagonally across the hillside for over two kilometres and peters out in the bogs at the foot of Drysgol. GR 873212. This peak is an undulating, grassy spur extending eastwards from the reigning peak, Aran Fawddwy.

Route 49. Dinas Mawddwy and Drysgol. Leave Dinas Mawddwy by the road to Bwlch y Groes and note the sparkling cascades of the Dyfi R. On reaching Aber Cywarch turn L and on emerging from the hedgerows beyond the cottages, cross the green strath to Cae Peris. The farm is splendidly situated amid a circle of green hills, but on the west is overhung by the black, forbidding cliffs of Craig Cywarch. Parking is only possible on the common at GR 854184. This criterion must be strictly observed otherwise access to this lovely area may be put in jeopardy. Park respectfully on the common in such a way as to not obstruct the flow of traffic and walk north to the bridge at GR 853187. Cross the bridge and follow the path which is clearly marked. This rises at an easy gradient for two kilometres and is cushioned with springy turf and fringed with golden sedge. Plod along steadily and meanwhile note how the floor of Hengwm L recedes with every step until at the end of the path it is nearly 500 metres below. Observe also L on the other side of it the magnificent buttresses and gullies of Craig Cywarch, which are frequented by rock climbers.

Now keep to the wire fence across the maze of bog and later bear R for some outcropping rocks where a charming little pool lies on the level end of the spur. This point discloses for the first time on this ascent the shattered front of Aran Fawddwy to the north-west, together with the cliffs of Aran Benllyn above the grassy spur in the centre of the ridge, as well as Creiglyn Dyfi far below held firmly in the grip of the hillside by a bulge in the grassy slope.

Drysgol narrows considerably as it bends round the head of Hengwm and at one spot, where a gully falls precipitously to the south, it is so narrow that the edge has given way. This coign of vantage is a good one for the appraisal of the shattered front of Aran Fawddwy, riven with gullies and surmounted by a cairn which is clearly silhouetted against the sky.

Continue the walk past the cairn on Drws Bach, erected in 1961 by the RAF (SAC Michael Robert Aspin of the RAF Mountain Rescue was killed by lightning here), cross the narrow ridge and begin to turn north along the edge of the precipices. Climb the broken rocks that rise to the first cairn, or if preferred, avoid them by going farther L to pick up a sheep track that mounts over grass. On attaining the crest of the ridge the reigning peak is disclosed on the skyline about half a mile to the north. Make your way through the chaotically arranged boulders and on reaching the summit cairn sit down to eat lunch and admire the spacious panorama.

Since the Arans are the most easterly peaks in Mid-Wales it follows that the most interesting views are round the western arc. Cadair Idris is seen almost end-on with the Harlech Dome R. Then come the peaks of Snowdonia and the isolated Arenigs that rise from the swelling moorland. Aran Benllyn is prominent at the end of the summit ridge, with R, Creiglyn Dyfi below, beyond this rise the vast moors of the Berwyns.

Walkers who are making the traverse of this group must now continue along the ridge to Aran Benllyn and then walk downhill all the way to Llanuwchllyn and eventually to Bala.

Should anyone wish to make the traverse in the reverse direction you must leave transport by the side of Pont y Pandy, in Llanuwchlyn. Follow the track towards Plas Morgan GR 880278, where signs direct you L up to the ridge. Its west side is then followed all the way to the summit of Aran Benllyn.

There is only one alternative route to the ridge and it starts at the National Park car park on the site of the disused railway station at Drws y Nant on the A494 where all cars must be parked. Walkers then follow the public right of way from Esgair Gawe Farm, GR 815223, on through the forest breaking on the west side of the ridge in the vicinity of Camddwr.

Access to this area is the subject of a complex agreement between landowners and the National Park Authority. Each access point to the mountains has a sign outlining the restrictions and visitors are asked to adhere to the guidelines. There is no camping, nor are dogs allowed in the area.

Plate 222 **Route 49**—Craig Cywarch seen from **Route 49**

Plate 224 **Route 49**—Creiglyn Dyfi—Birthplace of the river Dovey

Plate 226 **Route 49**—The Ridge to Aran Benllyn

Plynlimon

Pen Plynlimon Fawr   752 metres   2468 feet

OS Map: Landranger 135 Aberystwyth

Plynlimon is one of the three chief mountains of Wales, the others, as already noted, being Snowdon and Cadair Idris. The vast plateau extends from south-west to north-east and consists of grit and shale overlaid with coarse grass and bog, in fact satirists have described it as a "sodden weariness". However, this great dome is the source of the rivers Severn, Wye and Rheidol, and its slopes also give birth to several lesser but noteworthy streams. It was Owain Glyndower's lair in 1401, from where he sallied forth to harry the land.

There are two popular routes to the summit: that from Dyffryn Castell Hotel GR 774817 is longer and 4 kilometres of a broad, gradually rising ridge; that from the Farm of Eisteddfa Gurig GR 798841 is about half the distance and threads a wild valley to an abandoned lead mine, to rise thereafter direct to the cairn on the summit.

Walkers who visit this region solely to ascend Plynlimon could do no better than stay at Dyffryn Castell Inn, which has ten bedrooms and a bathroom, and is right on the spot for the walk. There is a larger hotel in Ponterwyd, some two kilometres distant, and another at the Devil's Bridge that is 5 kilometres away. The latter has the advantage of proximity to the Rheidol Valley, a magnificently wooded basin immediately opposite, which affords charming walks for those who come to explore the district. There is accommodation at Eisteddfa Gurig.

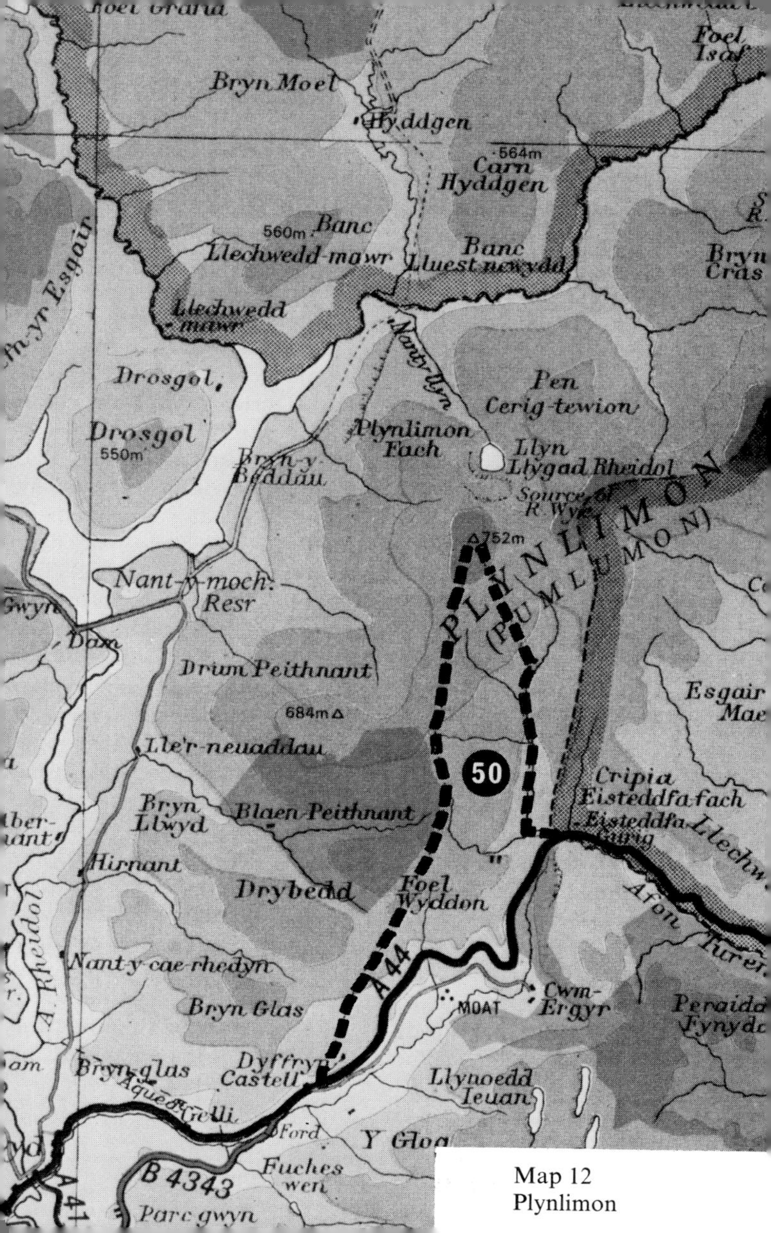

Map 12
Plynlimon

Route 50. From the Devil's Bridge. The drive to the foot of Plynlimon is pleasant and by taking the R fork B4343, at Tyn-y-Ffordd the road attains the 300 metre contour and hereabouts opens up the only good view of the mountain. Thereafter it descends in graceful curves, eventually to merge with the main highway just short of Dyffryn Castell, where there is a car park in front of the hotel. From here the road rises at an easy gradient along a wide, desolate valley, with the lofty grass ridge leading to the peak L, but the monotony of the landscape is relieved here and there by a few larches, which, however, disappear all too soon and are replaced by extensive spruce plantations away to the R. Eisteddfa Gurig stands at a bend on the crest of the pass and cars may be parked nearby.

Pass through two gates R of Dyffryn Castell and then bear L to climb the steep grassy slopes of the ridge immediately overhead. On attaining its crest bear R at an easier gradient and keep the valley in view R while ascending gradually over grass, heather and bracken for about three kilometres. The route follows the edge of the forest plantation to its north-eastern corner from where you can strike out slightly east of north for the summit.

When compared with the views from other peaks in Wales, that from Plynlimon is disappointing owing to the immensity of the moorland plateau in the vicinity, which seemingly diminishes its real height. The only mountains of note in the extensive panorama are Cadair Idris and the Arans away to the north.

Eisteddfa Gurig stands on the 400 metre contour and the ascent to the summit of Plynlimon involves a climb of only 350 metres. Pass through the farmyard and follow the disused track all the way to the lead mine GR 797857 first beside a playful stream with chattering cascades here and there and then north through great expanses of boggy moorland. From the lead mine climb steadily west of north to the summit cairn. There is absolutely nothing to relieve the monotony of the landscape on this route: no trees to break the skyline, no colourful flowers to carpet the wayside, no birds to charm both ear and eye, just the green and brown of grass and bog. Incidentally, both routes are much more pleasant going after a dry spell.

A correspondent who knows this region intimately suggests the following alternative approaches which he says are more interesting.

Drive or walk from Ponterwyd past Nantymoch reservoir to the small holding of Brynybeddau GR 775882 Maesnant then proceed up the remote valley of the Afon Hengwm. One of three routes can then be chosen, depending on time and inclination:

1 Head for Llyn Llygad Rheidol GS 7987 and ascend through grassy crags to the summit of Plynlimon Fawr.
2 Turn up Cwm Gwerin GS 8088 to the top of Pen Plynlimon Arwystli GR 816878 and walk along the ridge to the dominating summit.
3 Follow the stream almost to Llyn Bugeilyn GS 8292 and then attain the ridge to walk back southwards and then west, passing the source of the River Severn GS 8289 *en route*.

Plate 228 **Route 50** starts at Dyffryn Castell

Plate 230 The shorter variation of **Route 50** begins at Eisteddfa Gurig

The Black Mountains

Waun Fach	811 metres	2660 feet
Pen y Gadair Fawr	800 metres	2624 feet
Pen y Manllwyn	762 metres	2500 feet
Pen Allt Mawr	719 metres	2358 feet
Pen Trumau	707 metres	2320 feet
Twyn Tal-y-cefn	701 metres	2303 feet
Chwarel y Fan	679 metres	2228 feet
Pen y Beacon	676 metres	2219 feet
Pen Gloch-y-Pibwr	673 metres	2210 feet
Mynydd Llysiau	662 metres	2173 feet
Pentwynglas	645 metres	2115 feet
Black Hill	640 metres	2102 feet

OS Map: Landranger 161
         Outdoor Leisure 13 Brecon Beacons East

The Black Mountains cover an area of about 207 square kilometres to the north of Abergavenny. They consist largely of bleak whale-back ridges running from south-east to north-west and are dominated by the Gadair Ridge, which is crowned by Waun Fach, the highest peak in the whole group.

Three long valleys penetrate the fastnesses of the range: the Vale of Ewyas is the longest and most beautiful and is graced by the venerable ruin of Llanthony Priory. All the valleys follow roughly parallel lines in a north-westerly direction and terminate in the shadow of a broken ridge which connects all four of the main ridges. These ridges and valleys are excellent walking country and a variety of routes may be worked out. It is however, important to know some of the landmarks with certainty, owing to the very slight differences in height of a few of the peaks. This is not always apparent unless they are seen from afar and a case in point is that of the dominating Gadair Ridge where the difference in height between Waun Fach and Pen y Gadair Fawr is only eleven metres. When traversing the ridge this is not very clear save perhaps from the latter top, but it is quite apparent when observed from the highest parts of the Allt Mawr Ridge, over four kilometres to the south. When making the following ascent these features are worthy of note, and on attaining Waun Fach its summit will reveal the immensity of the range and perhaps induce the walker to make a more detailed exploration.

Route 51. The Gadair Ridge. A convenient starting point for this ascent is the sequestered hamlet of Pen y Genfford which stands at the highest point of the A479 between Crickhowell and Talgarth. There is parking near the site of the ruined castle at GR 177303. Walkers who approach it from the south will note the lofty ridge of Pen Allt Mawr which hems in the valley R almost all the way from Crickhowell. A glance at the map will show that Y Grib GR 193311 is the key to this route, and the foot of its ridge is reached by following an old farm track which passes round the north side of Castell Dinas. Advance along it for nearly a kilometre and then take a direct line for its conspicuous spur seen on the skyline ahead. On attaining its narrow crest, climb its sharp undulations and make for Pen y Manllwyn, a broad grassy top at the northern extremity of the Gadair Ridge. Then turn R and walk for just over 1.5 kilometres in a southerly direction to Waun Fach GR 215300 the reigning peak of the group. This lofty viewpoint unfolds an extensive panorama, in which the Brecon Beacons will draw the eye to the distant south-west, but the nearer whale-back ridges of the group are so immense that they obscure the deep valleys of the range. It also reveals the strange hump of Pen y Gadair Fawr GR 229287 over a mile to the south-east and its summit, crowned by a large cairn, may be reached by picking one's way carefully across the intervening boggy ground.

Map 13
The Black Mountains

Plate 231 The Black Mountains from Skirrid Fawr

Plate 232 **Route 51**—The dominating remnant of
Llanthony Priory

Plate 234 **Route 51**—Pen y Gadair and the Sugar Loaf from Waun Fach

The Brecon Beacons

Pen y Fan	886 metres	2906 feet
Corn Du	873 metres	2864 feet
Cribyn	795 metres	2608 feet

OS Map: Landranger 160
Outdoor Leisure 11 Brecon Beacons Central

Every walker bent upon the exploration of this beautiful group of hills should first visit the National Park Visitor centre GR 977263. The Centre is situated on a hill, and on the edge of an extensive stretch of mountain moorland known as Mynydd Illtud, which is separated from the Brecon Beacons by the Tarell Valley. The views in all directions are delightful and there is a cafe on site. The supervisor and assistant are usually available and willingly give information about the National Park which is admirably illustrated by an excellent display of maps, photographs and relevant literature. The Centre is undoubtedly one of the finest in the country.

These mountains form a compact and shapely group that is situated about mid-way between the Black Mountains on the east and Fforest Fawr and Carmarthen Fan on the west. Pen y Fan is the loftiest peak in South Wales and is a conspicuous object when seen from afar. The group is particularly attractive when viewed from the north, and the dominating peak assumes spectacular proportions when seen from the adjacent rib of Bryn Teg.

The easiest and quickest way to traverse the Brecon Beacons is from the Storey Arms, GR 983204, which stands at a height of 435 metres on the crest of the pass carrying the main road south from Brecon to Merthyr Tydfil. Mere peak-baggers may be satisfied with this short ascent but those who wish to see the real beauty of the group will miss much of it by doing so, and if they are also interested in photography and prefer, as they should, the most favourable lighting throughout, then they will follow the route described and illustrated herein.

The only snag for those without transport is that the complete circuit is a long one based upon Brecon and involves some 19 kilometres of walking, depending upon such diversions as are made to toy with a camera. It is possible to drive due south from the town for five kilometres where the road ends with space for a few cars, and this would reduce the walking distance to 10 kilometres. To reach this spot cross the bridge over the River Usk and then turn L off the highway at a church GR 038284; the road is narrow but well surfaced, thereafter to rise gradually in a southerly direction to end near the farm Bailea. GR 039240.

I first explored the Brecon Beacons in 1946 and Route 52 was then unknown, as Pen y Fan was always reached from the Storey Arms. Three years later I published a description of it in *Wanderings in Wales* and for over forty-five years so many walkers have followed in my footsteps that it has become the most popular route. Bryn Teg was then a bare grassy hill, with no path to the Cribyn, whereas today, after thousands of boots have climbed the Rib, it has been transformed into an easy staircase. Nevertheless, since its steepness has deterred legions of walkers, they have trodden a level path which goes off to the R and ends at the Col between Cribyn and Pen y Fan, so eliminating the only section of hard going in these hills.

Note – Walkers who decide to make the ascent from the Storey Arms should ascend the path behind the telephone box GR 983203, keeping the forestry on the right. Continue over Y Garn and skirt northwards around Blaen Taf Fawr to the Tommy Jones obelisk GR 000218. From here ascend Corn Du then turn north-east to Pen y Fan. The return descent can either be the reverse or from Bwlch Duwynt GR 005209 down to the

Gåer

Wern-fawr

312m

Bolgoed

Pen-y-parc

Illtyd

Tair-Bull

uadd-cwm-Camlais

Mynydd

MOUNTAIN
CENTRE

Afon Tare

CASTLE MOUND

+

Libanus

Felin-Camlais

Bryn-bolgoed

Mo

A4215

Glyn

Tarell

Llwch

Forest Lodge

Cwm-Llwch

Pen Milan

rynach

Cwr

m Frynych

n Craig Cerrig Gleisiad

Llwyn-y-celyn

Llyn Cwm Llwch

garth

627m

Gleisiad

A 470

Y Gyrn

BRECO

BEACO
(BANNA
BRYCHEINIC

t y Gwair

824m

A 470

489m

Bryn Du

ant Mawr

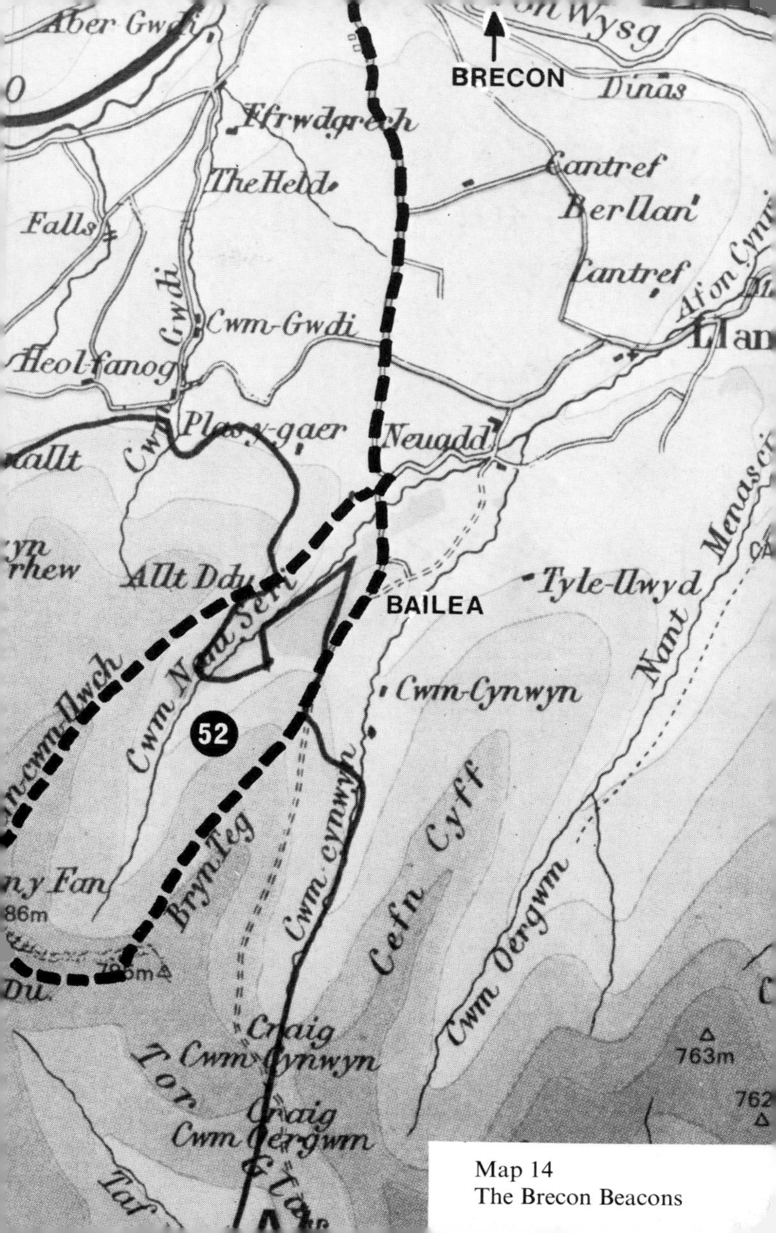

Map 14
The Brecon Beacons

Pont ar Daf lay-by GR 987198 about a kilometre south east of Storey Arms, where there are toilets.

Route 52. Bailea and Pen y Fan. Go along the stony track beyond the parking space. Go through a gate and ascend the slopes of the grassy ridge to the crest with the cliffs of Pen y Fan R, and take a direct line for the steep rib of Bryn Teg which culminates in the peak of Cribyn. This is continuously steep and the going is hard for a while, but on reaching its summit the rewards are immense: for the full stature of Pen y Fan is now revealed in all its grandeur, its precipitous front seamed with sinuous gullies and ribbed with grass and moss to afford a picture of mountain beauty. Now descend to the Col above Craig Cwm Sere and climb to the summit of Pen y Fan, meanwhile noting R its flat top supported by blocks of red sandstone lying end-on and poised above the innumerable layers of the same rock which alternate with successive bands of bright red earth.

On the summit is a cairn marking the site of a Bronze Age burial chamber and the view up an extensive panorama in which the vast bulk of the Black Mountains appear to the east and the peaks of Fforest Fawr lead the eye to Carmarthen Fan in the west. From Pen y Fan descend the grassy spur of Cefn Cwm-llwch to Allt Ddu, GR 027241. It is important to follow the correct path from here. There is a gate at GR 030247. Pass through the gate and on reaching the lane turn right to go through Plas y Gaer Farm. From here follow footpaths and lanes back to the point of departure.

Cribyn

Bryn Teg

Pen-y-Fan

Plate 237 **Route 52** from Cribyn

Plate 238 **Route 52**—Corn Du from Pen y Fan

Plate 239 **Route 52**—Llyn Cwm-Ilwch from Corn Du

Carmarthen Fan

Bannau Brycheiniog	802 metres	2632 feet
Bannau Sir Gaer	749 metres	2457 feet
Bwlch y Giedd	730 metres	2400 feet
Fan Hir	721 metres	2366 feet

OS Maps: Landranger 159
Outdoor Leisure 12 Brecon Beacons West

Known as the "Lost" mountain, this peak is situated nineteen kilometres due west of the Brecon Beacons, and in plan is rather like a gigantic isosceles triangle based on a line drawn westwards from the Gwyn Arms on the A4067. It dominates over 150 square kilometres of swelling moorland which is seamed with cascading streams, some of which disappear into the limestone. As a grassy eminence, the southern slopes of these lonely hills rise steeply at first and later at a more gentle gradient, finally to culminate in the shelter on Fan Brycheiniog GR 825218. The eastern ridge, a precipitous red escarpment, is nearly 6 kilometres in length and fringed with broken crags that drop away steeply to the moorland. It continues in an almost straight line, first to Fan Hir and after a conspicuous break at Bwlch y Giedd, to the pointed Fan Foel. The north-western rim is equally rosy and precipitous, but broken up into wild cwms. Two blue tarns grace the most northerly slopes of the mountain: to the east Llyn y Fan Fawr lies 200 metres below the summit, cradled in green hillocks; while to the west Llyn y Fan Fach lies at the foot of the frowning cliffs of Bannau Sir Gaer. There is only one hiatus in the eastern ramparts where a track, known as the Staircase, rises diagonally from the foot of the tarn to give easy access to the summit by way of Bwlch y Giedd GR 829214. Each of the north-western cwms carries a steep path: the first to the west of Fan Foel starts at Llanddeu-sant and swings round near the source of the Usk GS 8123 to rise in zig-zags to the ridge, but erosion has now made this ascent very arduous; the second to the east of Bannau Sir Gaer is in good condition and follows the Afon Sychlwch to its source at Pant y Bwlch GR 816219, the third starts from the waterworks at spot height 264m, keeps to the Afon Sawdde and passes to the west of the tarn to attain the end of the ridge.

The most comprehensive view of Carmarthen Fan is revealed from the old road running north beside the River Tawe from A4067 to Trecastle, whereas the western cwms are seen at their finest from spot height 458m on the path from Llanddeusant to the ridge. Both viewpoints may be conveniently reached from Trecastle by taking the road to Pont ar Hydfer GR 863276 where you turn L for the former. For the latter, continue to the Cross Inn GR 773258 where you turn L for the church and again L for spot height 254m.

It will be evident from the foregoing that although Carmarthen Fan is the highest peak in South-western Wales, its situation in an often boggy and empty moorland has led to its being cold shouldered by walkers. However, this has helped to preserve it from the usual mountain scars and litter, and moreover, to retain its reputation as an unspoiled peak.

The most striking features of this mountain are all revealed near its summit; the rest of its topography lacks interest and is rough sloping moorland, and anyone caught here in bad weather, may have great difficulty in finding the exits.

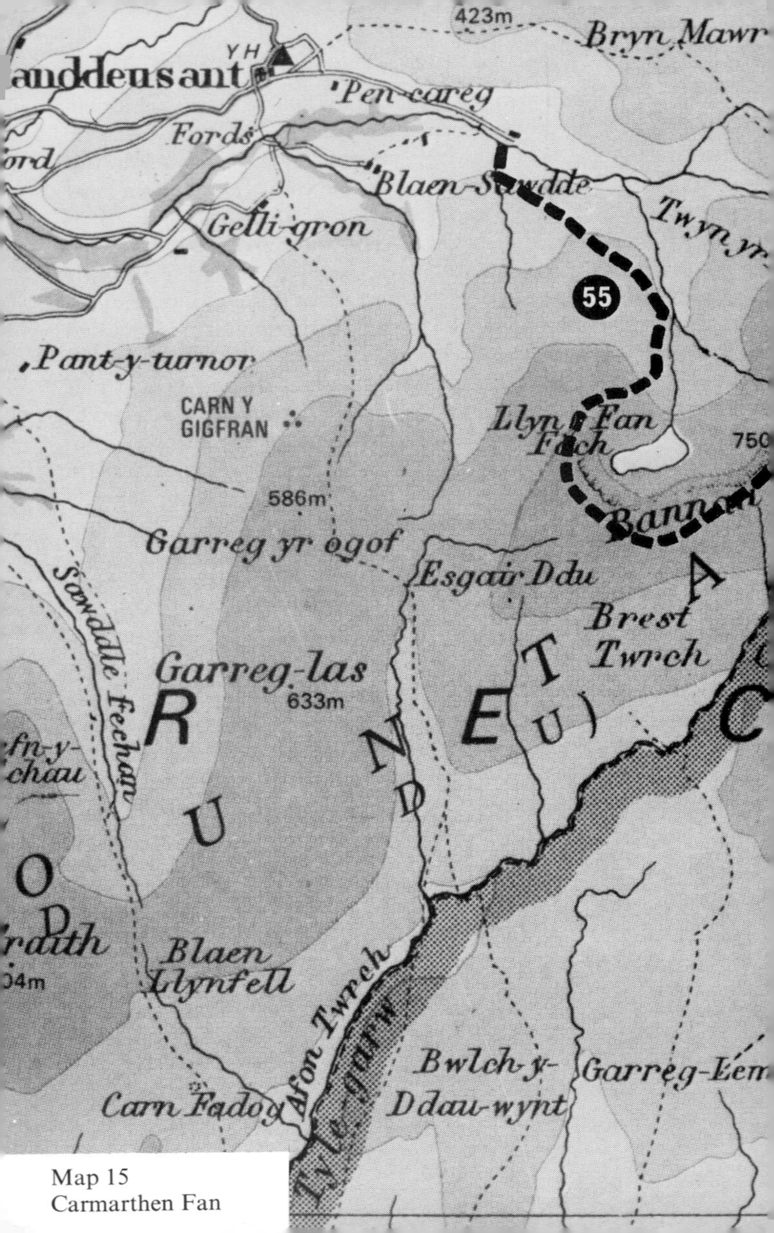

Map 15
Carmarthen Fan

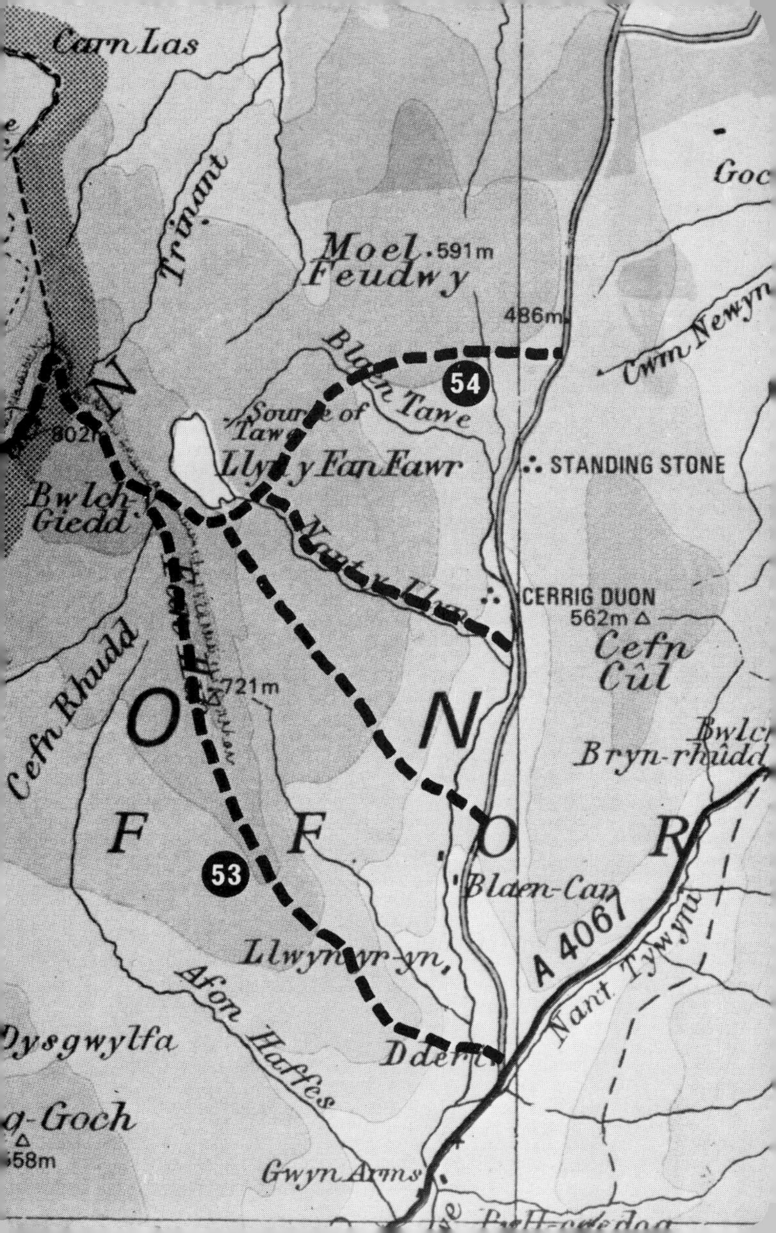

Carn Las

Trinant

Moel Feudwy .591m

486m

Goc

Cwm Newy

Blaen Tawe

54

Source of Taw

Llyn y Fan Fawr

STANDING STONE

N

Bwlch Giedd

802

Nant Tawe

CERRIG DUON
562m △

Cefn Cûl

Cefn Rhudd

O

721m

F

F

N

O

Bwlc
Bryn-rhudd

R

53

Blaen-Cau

A 4067

Llwyn-yr-yn

Nant Tywni

Afon Haffes

Dysgwylfa

Dderi

△
558m

g-Goch

Gwyn Arms

Fan Hir

Bwlch y Giedd

Bannau Brycheiniog

Fan Foel

Route 53. Gwyn Arms and Fan Hir. This mountain may be climbed by a variety of routes and that from the south begins at Tafarn y Garreg where a bridge over the River Tawe GR 848172 gives access to a path which is forsaken at the first farm. The hillside is ascended by bearing north-west. The eastern escarpment is reached and then followed to the summit cairn; it is the least interesting approach and just a continuous grind over grass. The car may be parked at the Gwyn Arms on a side road, or at the nearby church on the main road.

Route 54. Bwlch y Giedd. The key to the ascents and their alternatives from the Trecastle road is this pass. Our route begins just below the crest of Bwlch Cerrig-duon, beside a conspicuous metal sheepfold GR 855223 spotheight 476m. This is not far from the Standing Stone on the adjacent hillside and might well be described as THE STANDING STONE ROUTE. It begins with an almost level sheep track and later easy moorland slopes lead to the tarn. Now climb the Staircase from its southern end, and after passing three large cairns on the grassy slopes above it, bear R for the summit where a circular shelter provides protection from the elements on a wild day. Continue your walk to Fan Foel GR 824220 which is a better viewpoint because it unfolds the whole of the vast northern arc to perfection. To the east the Brecon Beacons top the distant skyline; to the north the moorland drops away to a forest of trees and a reservoir; while in the west are the cwms still to be reached. Continue your walk west along the edge of the lofty escarpment and note the magnificent elevation of Bannau Sir Gaer, the summit being Picws Du 749m, beyond which you will reach the cwm cradling the second tarn. Return the same way or take a compass bearing on Bwlch y Giedd GR 829214 and cross the moor to the aforementioned cairns, and so back to your car. The time required for this route is about five hours of easy going which allows time to view the scenery, eat your lunch and play with your camera. There are other variations to

Plate 242　The summit of Bannau Brycheiniog

this route beginning from the road along the way to the start mentioned here. Parking is possible at the roadside and in lay-bys but you must try to park considerately.

Route 55. Llanddeusant. This hamlet is the starting point of the northern approach to Carmarthen Fan and follows the road going east from the church to the waterworks beyond Blaenau Farm, from which point the view of the mountain is obscured by Twyn yr Esgair. There is ample parking at GR 799238. Do not continue further along the track. The path to the tarn of Llyn y Fan Fach begins here and continues all the way to it beside the prattling Afon Sawdde. Pass to the west of the tarn and climb to the end of the escarpment which you follow all the way to the summit.

A possible approach from the south-west is centred at Dorwen, GR 773148 from where a line due north-east, avoiding the crags of Tyle Garw and later crossing the Afon Twrch, leads to Bannau Sir Gaer and Picws Du and Fan Foel.

Note: Much of the moorland hereabouts is common land, some of it being owned by the National Park. Although the OS map indicates few rights of way, the public are at liberty to roam on this vast bleak moor but obviously in proper consideration of those who work the land.

Plate 245 **Route 54**—Fan Foel from Bannau Brycheiniog

Plate 247 Llyn y Fan Fawr and the summit shelter from Fan Foel

Plate 249 Llyn y Fan Fach from Bannau Sir Gaer

Index